LIT UP INSIDE

Lit Up Inside
Selected Lyrics

VAN MORRISON

edited by EAMONN HUGHES
foreword by IAN RANKIN

FABER & FABER

First published in 2014
by Faber & Faber Ltd
Bloomsbury House
74–77 Great Russell Street
London WC1B 3DA

Typeset by Ian Bahrami
Printed in Germany by GGP Media GmbH, Pößneck

A CIP record for this book
is available from the British Library

ISBN 978-0-571-31619-9
LIMITED EDITION ISBN 978-0-571-31620-5
DELUXE EDITION ISBN 978-0-571-32198-8

10 9 8 7 6 5 4 3 2 1

For Shana, Éabha and Fionn

Contents

Foreword *by Ian Rankin*

On a windswept Scarborough beach, I started listening to Van Morrison.

I'd liked what I'd heard up to then, but I hadn't heard much. This was 1989 and I was toiling: a flat in Tottenham I shared with my wife and our cat; a writing career that wasn't exactly making waves; a ninety-minute each-way commute to my job as a hi-fi reviewer in a dank basement in Upper Norwood. One morning, as I fought my way on to the train, I felt my heart bursting through my chest. I was sweating and shaking, adrenaline surging. The train left without me and I headed to the doctor's surgery. Panic attacks, he said. Get out of London for a bit, if you can. I packed a few things, including my Walkman and a dozen Van Morrison cassettes – his record company was reissuing his early catalogue and had sent review copies. Tottenham Hale to King's Cross to York, where I stood on a platform staring at the departures board. Scarborough: I'd never been there. Ticket, train, and eventually an out-of-season bed and breakfast with no view. On with the headphones and down to the deserted seafront with *Veedon Fleece, Saint Dominic's Preview, Hard Nose the Highway* . . .

There were stories in the music, and characters and commentary. There was a search for the spiritual in the commonplace, the personal straining towards the universal. I smiled at 'chamois cleaning all the windows', trying to think of another great lyricist who would begin a song with the conjuring of such an everyday chore. But then windows *do* need to be cleaned, or else there's a lack of clarity. Amidst the poetry there was room for disenchantment and anger, too. 'The Great Deception' tackled politics, lazy ideals, and the recording industry. This was a music filled with beautiful visions, sung with passion and immaculate phrasing by a singer who was both of the world and rooted in a particular upbringing and landscape. My wife had grown up in Troubles-era Belfast, so I recognised some of the street names and the route-maps through the Irish countryside. Mind, I wasn't sure exactly what hard-nosing the highway actually meant, but I was getting an inkling.

When Van Morrison sang of standing on the threshold, I realised he could be talking for all of us, poised throughout our lives between what we have already experienced and what may lie ahead. I was trying to summon the courage to quit my job and try to write full-time, to leave London and go travelling. Maybe that would be the end of the panic attacks – I wouldn't know unless I took that first step over the threshold. Meantime, I turned my collar up against the elements and, when the music stopped, ejected one tape and replaced it with another. Great tunes and arrangements, impeccable musicianship and that inimitable voice – but the words were a vital part of the whole, even when the sentiment was a simple but joyous 'I'm in heaven when you smile'.

So anyway, after a few days alone with myself I had to return to London, where my wife and I began to draw up our escape plan. Nearly thirty years on, I still have those cassettes. Plus the CDs and some of the vinyl. (And my wife.) And Van Morrison has continued to write with lyricism, passion and clear-headed articulation. From 'Mystic Eyes' (1964–6) to 'Mystic of the East' (2012), there's a spiritual element throughout, but there are also stories teeming with incident and characters, and grand travelogues, and an extolling of life's simple pleasures – love and friendship, a quiet drink, silent empty spaces. In 1995's 'Songwriter' he implores his audience: 'Please don't call me a sage/I'm a songwriter.' And so he is, but not every songwriter's lyrics cast such a spell when stripped of the accompanying music. His words chart his life, from Belfast to Boston and beyond. You'll feel you know him more deeply after reading them. Better still, they'll lead you back into the music, music to warm the soul, just as it did on a freezing beach in Scarborough, one life-changing week in 1989.

Introduction *by Eamonn Hughes*

Any significant writer creates their own world. Van Morrison has certainly done this through his music, which, as the playwright Stewart Parker put it, is an 'amalgam of urban styles which Morrison has made his own'. This book exists because Morrison has also created a world through his words. It is a world of back streets and mystic avenues; memories of childhood wonder and of adult work suffuse it; it is a place where the chime of church bells and the playing of the radio break a silence that can be sometimes stifling, at other times spiritual. It is a world generously peopled (in all senses of that phrase), but solitude and the benefits of being 'cloud-hidden' are never overlooked. Here love exists but may not last in either its divine or earthly forms. It is a place of sharp dealing but also of consolation, comfort and even grace. It is a world bounded by the river and the railway line, though these are means of passage as much as boundaries. The river and the railway are key features of the lexicon of twentieth-century popular music but, in their opposition of the natural and the man-made, they also echo the famous definition by Louis MacNeice (himself influenced by various forms of popular music) of Belfast being located between the 'mountains and the gantries'. Belfast is, then, as good a name as any for the world that we find in Morrison's words, but, as with MacNeice's poetry and Parker's plays, though Belfast may begin as a real place, it is ultimately more important as a site of the imagination. As such, it is not confined to the actual city of that name but is instead a terrain that can expand and contract as creative needs dictate.

This volume is made up of about a third of Morrison's work over a fifty-year career, and it aims to be a representative selection of that work. It begins and ends with versions of Belfast: 'The Story of Them' and 'Mystic of the East'. These are rooted in the city in which Morrison was born and grew up, and to which he has returned. Those bare biographical facts tell us little, however, about how Belfast is made and remade throughout his writing. The Belfast that has appeared in so many headlines during Morrison's life has also generated more than its share of remarkable writers over the last fifty years, but Morrison can stand shoulder to shoulder with them as someone who has not merely described his city, but rather shaped and moulded it to his own artistic ends.

'The Story of Them', one of the earliest lyrics gathered here, demonstrates just how soon he was doing this and with what degree of originality. It provides a map of the city like no other before it (and few since). This is a lyric written from within the moment and presents a version of Belfast recorded nowhere else: it's a Belfast in which the move from the Spanish Rooms on the Falls to the Maritime Hotel, just off the city centre, acknowledges no sectarian division. Instead, in this version of Belfast it is long hair and perceived scruffiness which are the markers of difference: this is a city mapped by music. While this may seem unremarkable – popular music in all its forms has, after all, consistently used place names – in the post-war years when America began to export new and exciting forms of music it was hard, on the eastern seaboard of the Atlantic, not to associate the originality and excitement of that music with the places in which it was set. So the names roll through the music as it develops from Mississippi to Chicago, from Kansas City to Broadway, from Memphis to Detroit, from New Orleans to New York. What Morrison understood before almost anyone else was that such places were not remote for those writing about them; these were the streets, rivers, cities and landscapes outside their doors. This involved recognising the places of popular music not as the exoticised landscapes of a glamorously foreign America, but rather as the often ambivalently welcoming places within which lives are lived and find expression. Given this, the blues can then roll down Royal Avenue just as readily as along the Mississippi and into Chicago. Morrison was therefore ahead of many of his contemporaries – Lennon and McCartney, Ray Davies, Jagger and Richards – in making lyrical use of his own place. (Chuck Berry, after all, wrote about Liverpool before the Beatles did.) To say that Morrison invented a Lagan Delta may seem improbable until one remembers that Belfast is a city of many rivers – the Beechie, the Connswater and the Lagan are all named in his songs – and these are matched by the variety of music that flows through its streets in his imagining of it. This intuition about place is all the more remarkable when one thinks of the history of poetry in Belfast and Northern Ireland. The story of that poetry often involves a search for predecessors who can, in the face of pressure from metropolitan centres, enable the use of a local territory for imaginative purposes; so Seamus Heaney looks back to Patrick Kavanagh, just as Paul Muldoon looks back to Heaney. Morrison, under the considerable cultural pressure of the emergence of a new, American-oriented popular culture and operating on his own terms, comes early to an understanding of the value of his own place, and is in turn then able to give expression to the experience of that place.

None of this is to say that Belfast is in any way a confined location. As with any deeply imagined terrain it has its specific features, yet can open out to encompass anything and everything that creativity may need to call on. It can be as small as a room or a backyard, or as open-ended as a threshold on to wonder. Even as he was asserting the right of the real Belfast as a fit location for his lyrics, Morrison was also beginning to see through and beyond it. Belfast is the first location for the visionary aspects of Morrison's writing as it moves from the everyday into the possibility of the extraordinary; from his earliest writing, back streets can turn into mystic avenues. The city is then made to yield to a form of what we have to call urban pastoral when transformed by everyday vision. In that phrase we also have to understand that the visionary is elevating and celebrating the everyday.

Belfast is also filtered through many song styles. The conventions governing the lyrics of the blues are different from those of the soul ballad and different again from the country-and-western song, to pick just three styles. In this volume these styles are to be seen in the different shapes that the lyrics make on the page, from the brevity and repetition of 'Mystic Eyes', through the rolling variations of 'Summertime in England' and the way in which the spoken section of 'See Me Through Part II' breaks into the regularity of the hymn form, to the formality on the page of 'Songwriter'. Each song style answers to different imperatives, satisfies different needs. In each instance, the writer has to balance the need to stay close enough to the convention to keep the style recognisable while also challenging and stretching those conventions. In Morrison's case the popular song, in whatever form, is constantly challenged and stretched: the aim, to adapt a phrase of Seamus Heaney's, is to make it eat stuff it has never eaten before. Partly because so many of the forms in which he works are, as he knows, deep-rooted, Morrison's voice has a maturity and an interest in matters which go beyond those usually thought of as the preserve of the song lyric.

In none of this, then, can we say that his writing is confined to a specific locale. In using Belfast (and, later, other Northern Irish places), Morrison's lyrics move in two directions: drilling down and back into origins and memories, and surging outwards in ever-expanding waves to other places and to that territory which is beyond place. On the one hand, the details of his city are associated with the many musics first heard there. These were both local (Orange bands, Salvation Army bands, gospel and praise music, hymns and folk music) and what we now think of as American (jazz, blues, rhythm and blues, gospel and soul). But the traffic between America and Belfast is long-standing. Emigrants from Ireland, many carrying their music with them, have been settling in America for centuries, and Belfast was one of the first places where the newly formed, post-revolutionary United States established a trade consulate. In the post-war period, as one of the war children, this connection was most obviously experienced by Morrison through records (and his father's collection has achieved almost legendary status), and even more particularly through the radio, which is, in its different guises – 'wireless', 'wavelength' and 'ether' are some of its other names in the songs – one of the recurrent features of Morrison's writing. It is always an immediate, even comforting presence: in that remarkable song 'T.B. Sheets', radio becomes the only possible consolation – 'I turned on the radio/If you wanna hear a few tunes, I'll turn on the radio for you/There you go, there you go, there you go, baby, there you go'. The radio in Morrison's writing is not the voice of some remote central authority, but rather an intimate presence bringing music from many different places (American music via European stations), and many of the features of that music, far from being in opposition to the 'Sunday-school culture' associated with local forms of music, have their roots in that culture. Radio and its correlates represent forms of connection, of both reception and transmission. The world outside comes sweeping in and is then sent rippling back out in a movement of contraction and expansion.

Morrison's recognition that the music which came to him through records and the radio has a kinship with and owes debts to the music of the streets, churches and tin tabernacles of his childhood enables him to distil the city into its abstract components – such as the train and the river (to take the title of Jimmy Giuffre's theme music from *Jazz on a Summer's Day*) – and use these to build a more expansive landscape. Belfast, too, can be taken and rendered into symbolic, even mythologised places. In this way Belfast is a constantly expanding territory: its borders are tested, its limits are stretched. So when the scene of the songs moves, as it does, to other places – London, Buffalo, Boston, San Francisco, England in summertime – it's not that they have nothing new to offer so much as that they are encountered as already familiar, known in advance and accepted for what they might add to the imaginative terrain. By the time of 'Saint Dominic's Preview', for example, 'the chains, badges, flags and emblems' of Belfast are seen to be on an equal footing with the archetypal blues location of the crossroads and the crying railroad trains of country music: 'And for every cross-country corner/For every Hank Williams railroad train that cries/And all the chains, badges, flags and emblems . . .'

Belfast, in Morrison's imaginative encounters with it, has an expansive quality, then, and while by no means all of his lyrics are to be thought of as literally located in the city and its environs – the room in 'Gloria' or the 'old graveyard' of 'Mystic Eyes' could be anywhere – it remains the foundational location, the place where music first played and thus enabled the expansion into all other places. So when Morrison's lyrics move outwards and away from Belfast, 'way up to Caledonia', say, that movement is both outwards towards a mythical pan-Scottish territory and yet carries with it the memory of Louis Jordan's 'Caldonia' (which Morrison has covered). The lyrics journey towards more recognisably American landscapes, but there is no sense of being either overawed or of simply offering the scale and unfamiliarity of these places as interesting in their own right. Instead there is a near-paradoxical sense of familiarity rooted in pre-existing knowledge derived from music and literature absorbed initially in Belfast: 'I heard Leadbelly and Blind Lemon/On the street where I was born/Sonny Terry, Brownie McGhee and/Muddy Waters . . ./I went home and read . . ./Kerouac's *Dharma Bums* and *On the Road*'. The songs of America, as we might call them, can, then, stand beside the deep American pastoral of *Basement Tapes*-era Bob Dylan and the first albums of The Band. Like them, though he has come from much further away, Morrison understands the deep roots of these songs and knows that the sweetness of Tupelo honey is given some of its savour by the bitterness of Tupelo blues.

The other element that enters the lyrics at this time, despite the temptations of American pastoral, is a hard-edged rejection of the too-easy comforts of a counter-culture peopled by those ultimately 'determined/Not to feel anyone else's pain'. The blandishments and deceptions of the music business are a frequent and justified target of Morrison's songs, distractions from the real work of being a 'Songwriter', which, as with cleaning windows in his youth, is a matter of being 'a working man in my prime'. Against the music business's sharp practices, we have to consider the generosity of Morrison's lyrics: they are richly populated by a cast of formative influences, cultural icons and contemporaries. Any reader of these words can acquire an extraordinary musical education simply by noting the names of other musicians and singers. What most of these names have in common is the fact that, confronted with a sharp-edged and often punitive world, they too sought for ways to express both the details of that world and to reach for something beyond it. Whether these figures are defined as blues or soul or rock-and-roll singers, their origins are most often in forms of sacred music. Consequently, in their music there is a frequently unresolved tension between celebrating such joys as are to be found in a hard, secular world and a striving to express something beyond that world. Looking at the many literary names that pepper such songs as 'Rave on, John Donne' in this context makes one realise that these writers are named too because they share this irresolution between the sanctified and the sinful.

No matter how specific his songs are, how rooted in this world, there is always that element of searching for that which lies beyond. It's there from the start in 'Mystic Eyes' (and could the name 'Gloria' really have been chosen at random? Like the greatest of soul songs there is an aching ambiguity in many of Morrison's lyrics as they slide back and forth between the sacred and secular) and it continues throughout his writing. There are songs here which reach, however uncertainly, for something which cannot be articulated. Another feature of the writing is just how often it courts silence. 'On Hyndford Street' (a phrase from which provides the title for these selected lyrics) is notable for its concern not only with the sounds but also the silences of Belfast. If Morrison's music is a compound of the urban sounds itemised here – the wireless playing Radio Luxembourg, the railway, 'Sunday six bells', 'Debussy', 'voices echoing late at night over Beechie River' – then the words are trying to capture, here and elsewhere, a kind of living silence. Anyone who has seen Morrison perform live will know that he plays with the full dynamic range available to him: he and his band can switch from full-throated roar to stealth mode, as if trying to play silence itself. His words, too, attempt this impossibility – silence runs through them. It's there in the last lyric collected here, 'Mystic of the East': 'I can't find any reason to speak'. But this song also returns us to the streets of 'Cleaning Windows', in which he is earning a living and, away from manual labour, developing interests in mysticism and music and literature. If Belfast is known for political violence and, prior to that, for being an industrial city, Morrison's words offer an alternative to the first and an all too rare glimpse of the second: accounts of physical labour are still remarkably rare in all kinds of writing. But what they also suggest is that even somewhere as apparently unpromising as industrial east Belfast, Morrison's original stamping ground, can be offered as a place of potential spiritual wonder. Taken as a whole, Morrison's words, then, offer those things that we look for in popular song, but they also offer so much more.

It is for others to interpret the details of these songs as they see fit, for others to argue the merits of those interpretations. Despite the temptations of such argument, what I've tried to offer here is a map of the world of Van Morrison's lyrics. Some will find it useful, I hope, as a guide to some of the features of that world. Others may well find it more pleasurable and instructive simply to get lost in this rich, expansive, many-peopled place, with its grittiness, its visions, its longing and loss, and its sense of deep fulfilment. Whichever way you choose to proceed, we can all, in this volume, follow the words as they 'rave on . . . on printed page'.

The Story of Them

When friends were friends
And company was right
We'd drink and talk and sing
All through the night
Morning came leisurely and bright
Downtown we'd walk
And passers-by
Would shudder with delight
Mmmmmm
Good times

At Izzie's, man
All the cats were there
Just dirty enough to say
'We don't care'
But the management had had complaints
About some cats with long, long hair
'Look, look, look'
And the people'd stare
'Why, you won't be allowed in anywhere'
Barred from pubs, clubs and dancing halls
Made the scene at the Spanish Rooms on the Falls
And, man, four pints of that stuff was enough to have you
Out of your mind
Climbing, climbing up the walls
Out of your mind
But it was a gas, all the same
Mmmmmm
Good times

Now just right about this time with the help of the three Js

Started playin' in the Maritime
That's Jerry, Jerry and Jimmy
And you know they were always fine
And they helped us run the Maritime
And don't forget Kit
Boppin' people on the head and knockin' them out
You know he did his bit and all
Was something else then
Mmmmmm
Good times

Now people say, 'Who are,
Or what are,
Them?'

That little one sings and that big one plays the guitar with a
Thimble on his finger, runs it up and down the strings
The bass player don't shave much
I think they're all a little bit touched
But the people came
And that is how we made our name
Too much, it was
Mmmmmm
Yeah, good times

Wild, sweaty, crude, ugly
And mad
And sometimes just a little bit sad
Yeah, they sneered and all
But up there, we just havin' a ball
It was a gas, you know
Lord
Some good times

We are Them, take it or leave it

Do you know they took it?
And it kept coming
And we worked for the people
Sweet sweat
And the misty, misty atmosphere
Gimme another drink of beer, baby
Gotta get goin' here
Because it was a gas
Lord
Good times

Blues come rollin'
Down all your avenue
Won't stop at the City Hall
Just a few steps away
You can look up at
Maritime Hotel
Just a little bit sad
Gotta walk away
Wish it well

Gloria

Like to tell you 'bout my baby
You know she comes around
Just about five feet four
From her head to the ground
You know she comes around here
Just about midnight
She make me feel so good, Lord
She make me feel alright

And her name is G–L–O–R–I–I–I–I
G–L–O–R–I–A – Gloria
G–L–O–R–I–A – Gloria
I'm gonna shout it all night
Gloria
I'm gonna shout it every day
Gloria

She comes around here
Just about midnight
She make me feel so good, Lord
She make me feel alright
Comes walkin' down my street
Comes up to my house
She knocks upon my door
And then she comes to my room
She make me feel alright
G–L–O–R–I–A
G–L–O–R–I–A

I'm gonna shout it all night
I'm gonna shout it every day

Yeah, yeah, yeah, yeah, yeah
It's so good
Alright
Just so good
Alright

My Lonely Sad Eyes

Fill me my cup
And I'll drink your sparkling wine
Pretend that everything is fine
Till I see your sad eyes
Throw me a kiss
Across a crowded room
Some sunny windswept afternoon
Is none too soon for me to miss my sad eyes
Not bad eyes or glad eyes
But you, my sad eyes

Fortunate and free
And there go you and I
Between the earth and sky
But who are you and I wonder why we do so?
My sad eyes
Lonely

Oh what a story
The moon in all its glory, the song I sing and everything
For you, my sad eyes

You'd better
Fill me my cup
And I'll drink your sparkling wine
Pretend that everything is fine
Till I see your sad eyes
Not bad eyes or glad eyes
But you, my sad eyes
My lonely sad eyes

Mystic Eyes

One Sunday mornin'
We went walkin'
Down by the old graveyard
In the mornin' fog
And looked into
Yeah

Those mystic eyes, mystic eyes, mystic eyes, mystic eyes
Mystic eyes, mystic eyes, mystic eyes, mystic eyes

Philosophy

Told you, darling, all along
I was right and you were wrong
Pleasin' you is so hard to do
Tried all night long to be true

Can't sow wild oats 'spect to gather corn
Can't take right and make it wrong
Told you, darlin', long time ago
You gotta reap what you sow
And what you sow, yeah
Gonna make you weep someday, someday, someday
Yeah, what you sow
Gonna make you weep

Tried to keep you satisfied
Broke my heart, hurt my pride
It's all over now s'far as I can see
It's a lonely road and a memory
Of daily walkin' and talkin' about you and me, can't you see
I said, daily walkin' and talkin'

Can't sow wild oats 'spect to gather corn
Can't take right and make it wrong
Told you, darlin', long time ago
You gotta reap what you sow
And what you sow, yeah
Gonna make you weep someday, someday, someday
Yeah, what you sow, yeah
Gonna make you weep
Someday

Brown Eyed Girl

Hey, where did we go, days when the rains came
Down in the hollow, playing a new game
Laughing and a-running, hey, hey
Skipping and a-jumping
In the misty morning fog with our, our hearts a-thumping
And you, my brown eyed girl
You, my brown eyed girl

Whatever happened, to Tuesday and so slow
Going down the old mine with the transistor radio
Standing in the sunlight laughing
Hiding behind a rainbow's wall
Slipping and a-sliding all along the waterfall
With you, my brown eyed girl
You, my brown eyed girl

Do you remember when we used to sing
Sha la la la la la la la la lala dee dah
Just like that
Sha la la la la la la la la lala dee dah
La dee dah

So hard to find my way, now that I'm all on my own
I saw you just the other day, my, how you have grown
Cast my memory back there, Lord
Sometimes I'm overcome thinking about
Making love in the green grass, behind The Stadium
With you, my brown eyed girl
You, my brown eyed girl

Do you remember when we used to sing

Sha la la la la la la la la lala dee dah
Laying in the green grass
Sha la la la la la la la la lala dee dah
Dee dah dee dah dee dah dee dah dee dah dee
Sha la la la la la la la la la la la la
Dee dah la dee dah la dee dah la

T.B. Sheets

Now listen, Julie baby
It ain't natural for you to cry in the midnight
It ain't natural for you to cry way into midnight through
Until the wee small hours long 'fore the break of dawn
Oh Lord

Now, Julie, an' there ain't nothin' on my mind
More further 'way than what you're lookin' for
I see the way you jumped at me, Lord, from behind the door
And looked into my eyes
Your little star-struck innuendos
Inadequacies and foreign bodies
And the sunlight shining through the crack in the windowpane
Numbs my brain
And the sunlight shining through the crack in the windowpane
Numbs my brain, oh Lord

Ha, so open up the window and let me breathe
I said open up the window and let me breathe

I'm looking down to the street below, Lord, I cried for you
I cried, I cried for you

Oh Lord

The cool room, Lord, is a fool's room
The cool room, Lord, is a fool's room
And I can almost smell your T.B. sheets
And I can almost smell your T.B. sheets
On your sick bed

I gotta go, I gotta go
And she said, 'Please stay, I wanna, I wanna,
I want a drink of water, I want a drink of water,
Go in the kitchen get me a drink of water'
I said, 'I gotta go, I gotta go, baby'
I said, 'I'll send, I'll send somebody around later,
You know we got Janet comin' around here later
With a bottle of wine for you, baby, but I gotta go'

The cool room, Lord, is a fool's room
The cool room, Lord, Lord, is a fool's room, a fool's room
And I can almost smell your T.B. sheets
I can almost smell your T.B. sheets, T.B.

I gotta go, I gotta go
I'll send around, send around one that grumbles later on,
    baby
We'll see what I can pick up for you, you know
Yeah, I got a few things going on too
Don't worry about it, don't worry about it, don't worry
Huh uh, go, go, go, I've gotta go, gotta go, gotta go, gotta go
Gotta go, gotta go, huh uh, alright, alright

I turned on the radio
If you wanna hear a few tunes, I'll turn on the radio for you
There you go, there you go, there you go, baby, there you go

You'll be alright too
I know it ain't funny, it ain't funny at all, baby
Always laying in the cool room, man, laying in the cool room
In the cool room, in the cool room

Spanish Rose

The wine beneath the bed
The things we've done and said
And all the memories that come glancing back to me
In my loneliness
Standing in the breach
The arms outstretched, but out of reach
And consciousness has found me sometimes wondering
Where you're at
Take me back again
Take me back one more time, Spanish rose

The way you pulled the gate
Behind you when you said, 'It ain't too late
Come on, let's swing the town and have a
Ball tonight'
And hoping you'd come through
And many others too
And all the friends we used to have in days gone by
I'm wondering
If you'll take me back again
Take me back one more time, Spanish rose

And when the lights went out
And no one was about, another country in full bloom
In the room we danced
And many hearts were torn
And when the word went around that everything was wrong
And just couldn't be put right
It tore me up, it tore me up, Lord

The way you held the note

The trembling in your throat
That just beginning of your wondrous smile
The rising of the water
The window into days gone by
I often ask myself and wonder why it's gone
Take me back again
Take me back one more time, Spanish rose

In slumber you did sleep
The window I did creep
And touch your raven hair and sang that song
Again to you
You did not even wince
You thought I was the prince
To come and take you from your misery
In lonely castle walls
Ah take me back again
Take me back one more time, Spanish rose

Who Drove the Red Sports Car?

Who drove the red sports car from the mansion
And laid upon the grass in summer time?
And who done me out high-time fashion
And made me read between the lines?
And who said, 'Follow the mile, you're only a child,
Sit on your throne, you got to make it on your own,
On your own'?

And who said, 'Ha, ha, look at you, look at you,
You got jam on your face'?
And who did your homework and read your Bible
And signed your name every place?
And who said, 'Fortunes untold don't go by gold,
You're much better known, you got to make it on your own,
On your own'?

And do you remember, do you remember this time?
I said a long time ago, when I came walkin' down
I came walkin' down, by Maggie's place
It started comin' on rain, it started comin' on rain
'Cause I had nothing on but a shirt and a pair of pants
And I was getting wet, I was getting wet, saturated, saturated
And Maggie opened up the window, and Jane swung out her
    right arm
She said, 'Hi!' I said, 'Hi, how're you doing, baby?'
She said, 'Come on in out the rain, come on in out the rain,
Lord, come on in out the rain, sit down by the fireside
And dry yourself.'
Achoo! Do it, do it, ha ha ha, I got caught
I got caught in a, in a bag, in the bag, oh Lord
I said, 'I don't mind if I do, I don't mind if I do'

Send Your Mind

Send your mind, send your mind
Send your mind, send your mind

While you're out there on the highway
Where the drivers roll on by
Going south between the bridges
Where the river's runnin' dry
And if you can't come home
Please send your mind

Send your mind, send your mind
Send your mind, send your mind

There you're talking, where you're going
On the train that ceased to roll
Across the nation, passing station
Where the night is black as coal
And if you can't come home
Please send your mind

Send your mind, send your mind
Send your mind, send your mind

With your hand laid on your heartbeat
And your head between the sheets
And the silence from the lamp post
On the corner of the street
And if you can't come home
Please send your mind

Send your mind, send your mind

Send your mind, send your mind
Send your mind, send your mind
Send your mind, send your mind

Ah little darlin', come on home
Come on home, ah send it, send it
Ah darlin', send it, baby
All you gotta do
Ah send it

The Back Room

In the back room, in the back room
I waited for you, you waited for me
The rain came down, pitter pat
Said, 'What, you think it's raining outside?'
Said, 'So what, turn the record player on'
Had a smoke, stood up, walked across to the john
In a cloud of mist, couldn't resist
Katie stepped in the hall, she grabbed the door
Found the key in the letterbox, she turned the door
Walked into the room, said, 'What's going on?

'I just got back from down the road,
I got a couple of bottles of wine, something to turn you on,
What'd you think about that?'
I said, 'Sit down, child,
Pull up a seat, you're soaking wet,
Take off your coat and hat, wipe your feet on the mat'
In the back room, in the back room
I waited for you, you waited for me

I said, 'What time it is, Johnny, where did we go all day?
Seem to get nowhere and do nothing
But sit looking at each other'
He said, 'I know, I've been doing the same thing for weeks'
I look at the clock and all of a sudden
I'm hypnotised and it speaks to me
And it goes tick-tock, tick-tock, tick-tock

And Katie said, 'I don't know what you gotta do
But I been working so hard lately
That I get home and just fall asleep in bed'

So we played some more sounds and grooved a while
Somebody brought out some cherry wine, cherry wine
And we talked about what was going on in the music world
And other things
Rain outside came down like it came never before
Down it came, down it came, rain, rain, rain
And I said, 'Baby, what time is it, what time is it,
Tell me, what time is it?'

'Four thirty'

So I peep round the corner of the blinds, and there you go
There's the little girls coming home from school
Looking so cool
Just learned their As to Zs
I said, 'Hey, man, don't that look funny, all of those girls
Coming home from school
And us sitting, talking and drinking
And all them other funny things?' Ha, ha

And Johnny said to me, 'You know what?'
I said, 'What?'
He said, 'Man, you gotta go out there and do something for
    yourself
You gotta go out and make
Or else you're gonna be sitting around here like nothing'
I said, 'You're right.' I said, 'You're so right'
He said, 'I know'
I said, 'Do ya?'
He said, 'You know you're cutting records, cutting records,
    right?
You can't do that and get through all the time.
You're gonna be out on the road
In the back seat, man, on the highway,
And the colours are gonna run.

All of a sudden don't you feel sick and the next day
You gotta make it?'
I said, 'Yeah, I feel sick'
I said, 'You know I can't stay here all the time,
As much as I'd like to
Just loon about all day and all night'
I decided to go down to the river
And watched the artist go through the motions

Gotta do my thing, gotta do my thing
In the back room, in the back room

Joe Harper Saturday Morning

When you thought I was a stranger
When you looked upon me
When I came back
But to take you from disaster
I cannot master the four winds in your shack
And the roamin' in the gloamin'
You have brought and set before me
And I think that it's an omen
I'm just not what so many people see

And you shined your glory all around
Did not disguise what you did
I asked you for half a pound, and you said
'Go see Joe Harper, Saturday morning, kid,
Go see Joe Harper, Saturday morning, kid'

And the child held the ball in the garden
With the old queen
And you kissed the lips that harden of a stranger
You know what I mean
And you walk down the streets so lonely
In your own childish way
And you thought that you would only
Do it for today

And you shined your glory all around
Did not disguise what we did
I asked you for half a pound, and you said
'Go see Joe Harper, Saturday morning, kid,
Go see Joe Harper, Saturday morning, kid'

And just outside the club
And the rain came down on his head
And he got all soaking wet
I said, 'Go for yourself,' and he said, 'I know, sure, sure,
I ain't conquered yet'
And I walked away from the backstreets in the rain and I saw
How many times that I die
And we turned on outside in the bus shelter
And I jumped on and said goodbye

And I shined my glory all around
Did not disguise what I did
Tried to keep it underground, but they said
'Go see Joe Harper, Saturday morning, kid,
Go see Joe Harper, Saturday morning, kid'

Madame George

Down on Cyprus Avenue
With the childlike visions leaping into view
Clicking clacking of the high-heeled shoe
Ford and Fitzroy and Madame George

Marching with the soldier boy behind
He's much older now, with hat on drinking wine
And that smell of sweet perfume comes drifting through
Early cool night air like Shalimar
And outside they're making all the stops
The kids out in the street collecting bottle tops
Gone for cigarettes and matches in the shops
Happy taking Madame George
Oh that's when you fall
Oh that's when you fall
Yeah, that's when you fall

When you fall into a trance
Sitting on a sofa playing games of chance
With your folded arms and history books you glance
Into the eyes of Madame George

And you think you've found the bag
You're getting weaker and your knees begin to sag
In a corner playing dominoes in drag
The one and only Madame George

And up from outside the frosty window raps
She jumps up and says, 'Lord have mercy,
I think that it's the cops'
And immediately drops everything she gots
Down into the street below

And you know you gotta go
On a train from Dublin up to Sandy Row
Throwing pennies at bridges down below
In the rain, hail, sleet and snow
Say goodbye to Madame George
Dry your eye for Madame George
Wonder why for Madame George

And as you leave, the room is filled with music
Laughing music, dancing music, all around the room
And all the little boys come round
Walking away from it all
So cool

And as you're about to leave
He jumps up 'n says, 'Hey, love,
You forgot your glove'
And the love that loves to love
That loves the love that loves
The love that loves to love
The love that loves to love
The love that loves

Say goodbye to Madame George
Dry your eyes for Madame George
Wonder why for Madame George
Dry your eyes for Madame George
Say goodbye

In the wind and the rain in the backstreet
In the backstreet
In the backstreet
Say goodbye to Madame George
In the backstreet
In the backstreet

In the backstreet
Well, down home
Down home in the backstreet
Gotta go
Say goodbye, goodbye, goodbye

Dry your eye, your eye, your eye
Your eye, your eye, your eye
Say goodbye to Madame George
And the love that loves to love
The love that loves to love

Say goodbye, goodbye, goodbye, goodbye
Say goodbye, goodbye, goodbye, goodbye
To Madame George
Dry your eyes for Madame George
Wonder why for Madame George
And the love that loves to love
The love that loves to love
Say goodbye, goodbye
Get on the train, darling
Get on the train, the train, the train, the train, the train,
    darling
This is the train, this is the train, darling
This is the train
Oh say goodbye, goodbye, goodbye
Get on the train
Get on the train

Slim Slow Slider

Slim slow slider
Horse you ride is white as snow
Slim slow slider
Horse you ride is white as snow
Tell it everywhere you go

Saw you walking
Down by Ladbroke Grove this morning
Saw you walking
Down by Ladbroke Grove this morning
Catching pebbles for some sandy beach
You're out of reach

Saw you early this morning
With your brand-new boy and your Cadillac
Saw you early this morning
With your brand-new boy and your Cadillac
You're going for something and I know you
Won't be back

I know you're dying, baby
And I know you know it too
I know you're dying
And I know you know it too
Every time I see you
I just don't know what to do

The Way Young Lovers Do

We strolled through fields all wet with rain
And back along the lane again
Staring at the sunshine, in the sweet summertime
The way that young lovers do

I kissed you on the lips once more
And we said goodbye at your front door
In the night-time
That's the right time
To feel the way that young lovers do

Then we sat on our own star
And dreamed of the way that we were
And the way that we wanted to be
Then we sat on our own star
And dreamed of the way that I was for you
And you were for me

And then we danced the night away
And turning to each other say
'I love you,
I love you'
The way that young lovers do

Then we sat on our own star
And dreamed of the way that we were
And the way that we wanted to be
Then we sat on our own star
And dreamed of the way that I was for you
And you were for me

And we learned to dance the night away
Turning to each other say
'I love you,
Baby, I love you'
The way that young lovers do
Lovers do
Lovers do

Moondance

Well, it's a marvellous night for a moondance
With the stars up above in your eyes
A fantabulous night to make romance
'Neath the cover of October skies
And all the leaves on the trees are falling
To the sound of the breezes that blow
And I'm trying to please to the calling
Of your heart strings that play soft and low
And all the night's magic seems to whisper and hush
And all the soft moonlight seems to shine in your blush

Can I just have one more moondance with you, my love?
Can I just make some more romance with you, my love?

Well, I wanna make love to you tonight
I can't wait till the morning has come
And I know now the time is just right
And straight into my arms you will run
And when you come my heart will be waiting
To make sure that you're never alone
There and then all my dreams will come true, dear
There and then I will make you my own
And every time I touch you, you just tremble inside
And I know how much you want me that you can't hide

Can I just have one more moondance with you, my love?
Can I just make some more romance with you, my love?

Well, it's a marvellous night for a moondance
With the stars up above in your eyes
A fantabulous night to make romance

'Neath the cover of October skies
And all the leaves on the trees are falling
To the sound of the breezes that blow
And I'm trying to please to the calling
Of your heart strings that play soft and low
And all the night's magic seems to whisper and hush
And all the soft moonlight seems to shine in your blush

Can I just have one more moondance with you, my love?
Can I just make some more romance with you, my love?

One more moondance with you, in the moonlight
On a magic night
In the moonlight
On a magic night
Can I just have one more moondance with you, my love?

Into the Mystic

We were born before the wind
Also younger than the sun
And the bonnie boat was one as we sailed into the mystic
Hark, now hear the sailors cry
Smell the sea and feel the sky
Let your soul and spirit fly into the mystic

And when that foghorn blows I will be coming home
And when the foghorn blows I want to hear it
I don't have to fear it
And I want to rock your gypsy soul
Just like way back in the days of old
And magnificently we will fold into the mystic

When that foghorn blows you know I will be coming home
And when that foghorn whistle blows I gotta hear it
I don't have to fear it
And I want to rock your gypsy soul
Just like way back in the days of old
And together we will fold into the mystic

C'mon, girl
Too late to stop now

Brand New Day

When all the dark clouds roll away
And the sun begins to shine
I see my freedom from across the way
And it comes right in on time
Well, it shines so bright and it gives so much light
And it comes from the sky above
Make me feel so free, make me feel like me
And it lights my life with love

And it seems like, and it feels like
And it seems like, and it feels like
A brand new day
A brand new day

I was lost, double-crossed
With my hands behind my back
I was long-time hurt and thrown in the dirt
Shoved out on the railroad track
I've been used, abused and so confused
And I didn't have nowhere to run
But I stood and looked
And my eyes got hooked
On that beautiful morning sun

And it seems like, yes, it feels like
And it seems like, yes, it feels like
A brand new day
A brand new day

And the sun shines down all on the ground
Yeah, and the grass is oh so green

And my heart is still and I've got the will
And I don't really feel so mean
Here it comes, here it comes
Here it comes right now
And it comes right in on time
Well, it eases me and it pleases me
And it satisfies my mind

And it seems like, yes, it feels like
And it seems like, yes, it feels like
A brand new day
A brand new day

Crazy Face

All the people were waiting for Crazy Face
He said he'd meet them at his favourite place
Dressed in black satin, white linen and lace
With his head held high and a smile on his face

And he said
'Ladies and gentlemen, the prince is late'
As he stood outside the churchyard gate
And polished up on his .38 and said
'I got it from Jesse James'

All the people were waiting for Crazy Face
He said he'd meet them in his favourite place
Dressed in black satin, white linen and lace
With his head held high and a smile on his face

He said
'Ladies and gentlemen, the prince is late'
As he stood outside the churchyard gate
And polished up on his .38 and said
'I got it from Jesse James'

I've Been Workin'

I've been workin'
I've been workin' so hard
I've been workin'
I've been workin' so hard
I come home
Make love to you, make love to you

I've been grindin'
I've been grindin' so long
I've been grindin'
I've been grindin' so long

Been up the thruway
Down the thruway
Up the thruway, down the thruway
Up, down, back up again

I said woman, woman, woman, woman, woman, woman,
    woman, woman
Make me feel so good
Woman, woman, woman, woman, woman, woman, woman,
    woman
Make me feel alright
Alright, alright, alright, alright
Alright, alright, alright, alright
Alright, alright, alright, alright
Alright, alright, alright, alright

I said woman, woman, woman, woman, woman, woman,
    woman, woman
Make me feel so good

Woman, woman, woman, woman, woman, woman, woman,
  woman
Make me feel alright
Alright, alright, alright, alright
Alright, alright, alright, alright
Alright, alright, alright, alright
Alright, alright, alright, alright

Make me feel so good
Set my soul on fire

Blue Money

The photographer smiles
Take a break for a while
Take a rest, do your very best
Take five, honey
Five, honey

Search in your bag
Light up a fag
Think it's a drag, but you're so glad
To be alive, honey
Live, honey

Say, when this is all over
You'll be in clover
We'll go out and spend
All of your blue money

Well, the cameraman smiles
Take a break for a while
Do your best, your very best
Take five, honey
Take five

Well, you search in your bag
Light up a fag
Think it's a drag, but you're so glad
To be alive, honey
Live, honey

Say, when this is all over
You'll be in clover

We'll go out and spend
All of your blue money

Say, when this is all over
We'll be in clover
We'll go out and spend
All your blue money

Blue money
Juice money
Loose money
Juice money
Loose money, honey
What kind of money, honey
Juice money
Loose money
Blue money

Street Choir

Street choir, sing me the song for the new day
Don't make it long and remember to sing it the old way
Let it all out, let your voice ring in the street now
My fun shall be this one to complete now

Why did you leave America?
Why did you let me down?
And now that things seem better off
Why do you come around?
You know I just can't see you now
In my New World crystal ball
You know I just can't free you now
That's not my job at all

Move it on up, move it on up by the window
Magnificent flow, let it all go in the moon glow
I'll take the wine, I'll take the wine with the gravy
Ask you the time and just send the bill to my baby

Why did you leave America?
Why did you let me down?
And now that things seem better off
Why do you come around?
You know I just can't see you now
In my new world crystal ball
You know I just can't free you now
That's not my job at all

Why did you leave America?
Why did you let me down?
And now that things seem better off

Why do you come around?
You know I just can't see you now
In my new world crystal ball
You know I just can't free you now
That's not my job at all
You know I just can't free you now
That's not my job at all

Tupelo Honey

You can take all the tea in China
Put it in a big brown bag for me
Sail right round all the seven oceans
Drop it straight into the deep blue sea

She's as sweet as Tupelo honey
She's an angel of the first degree
She's as sweet as Tupelo honey
Just like honey, baby, from the bee

You can't stop us on the road to freedom
You can't keep us 'cause our eyes can see
Men with insight, men in granite
Knights in armour bent on chivalry

She's as sweet as Tupelo honey
She's an angel of the first degree
She's as sweet as Tupelo honey
Just like honey, baby, from the bee

You can't stop us on the road to freedom
You can't stop us 'cause our eyes can see
Men with insight, men in granite
Knights in armour intent on chivalry

She's as sweet as Tupelo honey
She's an angel of the first degree
She's as sweet as Tupelo honey
Just like honey, baby, from the bee

She's alright, she's alright with me

You can take all the tea in China
Put it in a big brown bag for me
Sail it right round all the seven oceans
Drop it smack-dab in the middle of the deep blue sea

She's as sweet as Tupelo honey
She's an angel of the first degree
She's as sweet as Tupelo honey
Just like honey, baby, from the bee

Tell a tale of old Manhattan
Adirondack Trailways bus to go
And I'm waiting on my number
And I know my number's going to show

She's as sweet as Tupelo honey
She's an angel of the first degree
She's as sweet as Tupelo honey
Just like the real thing, from the bee

She's alright, she's alright with me

When that Evening Sun Goes Down

I want you to be around
When that evening sun goes down
I want you, be around
Keep my both feet on the ground
When that evening sun goes down
I want you, understand
Little girl, take me by my hand
I want you, understand
I wanna be your loving man
When that evening sun goes down

If it's nice, we'll go for a walk and a stroll in the clear moonlight
Singing a song, won't take long
Everything gonna be alright
And I wanna hold you oh so near
Keep you, darling, from all fear
I wanna hold you oh so near
Nibble on your little ear
When that evening sun goes down

If it's nice, go for a walk, stroll in the clear moonlight
Sing you a song, won't take long
Everything gonna be alright
And I wanna hold you oh so near
Keep you, darling, from all fear
I wanna hold you oh so near
Nibble on your little ear
When that evening sun goes down
When that evening sun goes down
When that evening sun goes down
When that evening sun goes down

Jackie Wilson Said (I'm in Heaven When You Smile)

Dadada da da da, dada da da da
Dadada da da da, dada da da da
Dadada da da da, dada da da da
Dadada da da da, dada da da da

Jackie Wilson said it was 'Reet Petite'
Kinda love you got, knock me off my feet
Let it all hang out, oh let it all hang out

And you know, I'm so wired up
Don't need no coffee in my cup
Let it all hang out, let it all hang out
Watch this

Ting-a-ling-a-ling, ting-a-ling-a-ling-ding
Ting-a-ling-a-ling, ting-a-ling-a-ling-ding
Do da do da do

I'm in heaven, I'm in heaven
I'm in heaven when you smile, when you smile
When you smile, when you smile

And when you walk across the room
You make my heart go, boom, boom, boom
Let it all hang out, baby, let it all hang out

And every time you look that way
Honey child, you make my day
Let it all hang out, what'd the man say, let it all hang out

Ting-a-ling-a-ling, ting-a-ling-a-ling-ding

Ting-a-ling-a-ling, ting-a-ling-a-ling-ding
Do da do da do

I'm in heaven, I'm in heaven
I'm in heaven when you smile, when you smile

I'm in heaven, I'm in heaven
I'm in heaven when you smile, one more time

I'm in heaven, I'm in heaven
I'm in heaven when you smile, when you smile

Gypsy

You can make out pretty good
When you're on your own
And you'll know just where you are
When you wanna roam

Got the moon above your head
And the road beneath your feet
Pull into a wooded glen
Make your own retreat

Li-a-di, di, di, di, di, di
Li-a-di, di, di, di, di, di
Li-a-di, di, di, di, di, di, di
Li-a-di, di, di, di, di, di
Li-a-di, di, di, di, di, di
Li-a-di, di, di, di, di, di, di
Gypsy

Laying underneath the stars
Can be so much fun
Especially when you're feeling good
When you're with the one you love

Sway to sounds of two guitars
Round the campfire bright
Then mellow out like violins
In the morning light

Li-a-di, di, di, di, di, di
Li-a-di, di, di, di, di, di
Li-a-di, di, di, di, di, di, di

Li-a-di, di, di, di, di, di
Li-a-di, di, di, di, di, di
Li-a-di, di, di, di, di, di, di
Gypsy

No matter where you wander
No matter where you roam
Any place you hang your hat
You know that that is home
Check it out first

Sway to sounds of two guitars
Round the campfire bright
Then mellow out like violins
In the morning light

Li-a-di, di, di, di, di, di
Li-a-di, di, di, di, di, di
Li-a-di, di, di, di, di, di, di
Li-a-di, di, di, di, di, di
Li-a-di, di, di, di, di, di
Li-a-di, di, di, di, di, di, di
Gypsy

Listen to the Lion

And all my love come down
All my love, come tumblin' down
All my love come tumblin' down
All my love, come tumblin' down

Oh listen to the lion
Oh listen, listen
To the lion
Sadly

And I shall search my soul
I shall search my very soul
And I shall search my very soul
I shall search my very soul

For the lion, for the lion
For the lion, for the lion
Inside of me

And all my tears have flown
All my tears, like water flow
And all my tears like water flow
All my tears, like water flow

For the lion, for the lion
For the lion, for the lion
Inside of me

Listen to the lion, listen to the lion
Listen to the lion, listen to the lion

And we sailed and we sailed
And we sailed and we sailed
And we sailed and we sailed
Sailed to Caledonia
And we sailed and we sailed
And we sailed and we sailed and we sailed
Way from Denmark, way up to Caledonia
Way from Denmark, way up to Caledonia
And we sailed and we sailed and we sailed
All around the world
And we sailed, and we sailed, and we sailed
Lookin' for a brand-new start
And we sailed, and we sailed, and we sailed
All around the world
Lookin' for a brand-new start, a brand-new start
Lookin' for a brand-new start, a brand-new start
And we sailed, and we sailed, and we sailed
And we sailed
Way from the Golden Gate
Way up to the New York City

Saint Dominic's Preview

Chamois cleaning all the windows
Singin' songs about Edith Piaf's soul
And I hear blue strains of 'Ne Regrette Rien'
Cross the street from Cathedral Notre Dame

Meanwhile back in San Francisco
I try hard to make this whole thing blend
And we sit upon this jagged
Story block with you my friend

And it's a long way to Buffalo
It's a long way to Belfast City too
And I'm hoping that Joyce won't blow the hoist
'Cause this time they bit off more than they can chew

As we gaze out on, as we gaze out on
As we gaze out on, as we gaze out on
Saint Dominic's Preview
Saint Dominic's Preview
Saint Dominic's Preview

All the orange boxes are scattered
Against the Safeway supermarket in the rain
And everybody feels so determined
Not to feel anyone else's pain

No one making no commitments
To anybody but themselves
Talkin' behind closed doorways
Trying to get outside empty shelves

And for every cross-country corner
For every Hank Williams railroad train that cries
And all the chains, badges, flags and emblems
And every strain on the brain and every eye

As we gaze out on, as we gaze out on
As we gaze out on, as we gaze out on
Saint Dominic's Preview
Saint Dominic's Preview
Saint Dominic's Preview

All the restaurant tables are completely covered
And the record company has paid out for the wine
You got everything in the world you ever wanted
And right about now your face should wear a smile

That's the way it all should happen
When you're in the state you're in
Have you got your pen and notebook ready
Think it's about time, time for us to begin

And meanwhile we're over in a 52nd Street apartment
Socialising with a wino few
I used to be hip and get wet with the jet set
But they was flyin' too high to see my point of view

As we gaze out on, as we gaze out on
As we gaze out on, as we gaze out on
Saint Dominic's Preview
Looked at the man
Saint Dominic's Preview
Looked at the band
Saint Dominic's Preview
Said their freedom marching out in the street
Freedom marching

Out in the street
Looked at the man
Turned around
Come back
Come back
Turned around
Looked at the man
Said, 'Hold on'
St Dominic's Preview
St Dominic's Preview
Soul meeting
St Dominic's Preview

Snow in San Anselmo

Snow in San Anselmo
And the deer cross by the lights
Of the mission down in old San Rafael
And a madman looking for a fight
A madman looking for a fight

And the massage parlour's open
And the clientele come and they go
And the classic-music station
Plays in the background soft and low
Plays in the background soft and low

And there's silence round the Cascades
And the air is crisp and clear
And the beginnings of the opera
Seem to suddenly appear
Seem to suddenly appear

And the pancake house is always crowded
Open twenty-four hours of every day
And if you suffer from insomnia
You can speed your time away
You can speed your time away

Snow in San Anselmo
My waitress, my waitress, my waitress
Said it was coming down
Said it hadn't happened in over thirty years
But it was laying on the ground
But it was laying on the ground

Warm Love

Look at the ivy on the old clinging wall
Look at the flowers and the green grass so tall
It's not a matter of when push comes to shove
It's just the hour on the wings of a dove
It's just warm love, it's just warm love

I dig it when you're fancy dressed up in lace
I dig it when you have a smile on your face
This inspiration's got to be on the flow
These invitations got to see it and know
It's just warm love, it's just warm love

And it's ever present everywhere, and it's ever present
    everywhere
That warm love
And it's ever present everywhere, and it's ever present
    everywhere
That warm love

To the country we're going
Lay and laugh in the sun
You can bring your guitar along
We'll sing some songs and have some fun

The sky is crying and it's time to go home
And we shall hurry to the car from the foam
Sit by the fire and dry out our wet clothes
It's raining outside from the skies up above
Inside it's warm love, inside it's warm love

And it's ever present everywhere, and it's ever present
   everywhere
That warm love
And it's ever present everywhere, and it's ever present
   everywhere
That warm love, can you feel it?

And it's ever present everywhere, and it's ever present
   everywhere
That warm love
And it's ever present everywhere, and it's ever present
   everywhere
That warm love

Hard Nose the Highway

Hey, kids, dig the first takes
Ain't that some interpretation
When Sinatra sings against Nelson Riddle strings
Then takes a vacation?

Seen some hard times, drawn some fine lines
No time for shoeshine, hard nose the highway

I was tore down at the Dead's place
Shaved head at the organ
But that wasn't half as bad as it was, oh no
Belfast and Boston

Seen some hard times, drawn some fine lines
No time for shoeshine, hard nose the highway

Put your money where your mouth is
Then we can get something going
In order to win you must be prepared to lose sometime
And leave one or two cards showing

Seen some hard times, drawn some fine lines
No time for shoeshine, hard nose the highway

Seen some hard times, drawn some fine lines
No time for shoeshine, hard nose the highway

Further on up the road
Further on up the road
It may not be today
It may be tomorrow

So if you live for today
Got to keep in mind
It may be tomorrow
Yes, further on up the road
Further on up
Further on up
Further on up
Further on up
Further on up
Further on
Up the road
Just might have to hard nose
Hard nose the highway
Hard nose the highway
Just might have to hard nose the highway
Hard nose the highway
Hard nose the highway
Further on

Further on
Further on up the road
I know you paid your dues in Canada
I know you paid your dues in Canada
But you just might
You just might have to hard nose
I hope not
I hope not
But you just might have to
I hope not
I hope not
But you just might have to hard nose
Hard nose the highway
Hard nose the highway

Wild Children

We were the war children
1945
When all the soldiers came marching home
Love looks in their eyes, in their eyes

Tennessee, Tennessee Williams
Let your inspiration flow
Let it be around while we hear the sound
Of the springtime rivers flow, rivers flow

Rod Steiger and Marlon Brando
Standing with their heads bowed on the side
Crying like a baby thinking about the time
James Dean took that fatal ride, took that ride

Tennessee Williams
Let your inspiration flow
Let it be around to hear the sound
When the springtime rivers flow, rivers flow

And Steiger and Marlon Brando
With their heads bowed on the side
Crying like a baby thinking about the time
James Dean took that fatal ride, took that ride

And we were the wild children
1945
When all the soldiers came marching home from war
With love looks, love looks in their eyes, in their eyes

The Great Deception

Did you ever hear about the great deception?
Well, the plastic revolutionaries take the money and run
Have you ever been down to Love City
Where they rip you off with a smile
And it don't take a gun?

Don't it hurt so bad in Love City
Don't it make you want to not bother at all?
And don't they look so self-righteous
When they pin you up against the wall?

Did you ever, ever see the people
With the teardrops in their eyes?
I just can't stand it, stand it no how
Living in this world of lies

Did you ever hear about the rock 'n' roll singers?
Got three or four Cadillacs
Saying, 'Power to the people, dance to the music'
Wants you to pat him on the back

Have you ever heard about the great Rembrandt?
Have you ever heard about how he could paint?
And he didn't have enough money for his brushes
And they thought it was rather quaint

But you know it's no use to heed it
And you know it's no use to think about it
'Cause when you start to think about it
You don't need it

Have you ever heard about the great
Hollywood motion-picture actor
Who knew more than they did?
And the newspapers didn't cover the story
Just decided to keep it hid

Somebody started saying it was an inside job
Whatever happened to him?
Last time they saw him down on the Bowery
With his lip hanging off an old rusty bottle of gin

Have you ever heard about the so-called hippies
Down on the far side of the track?
They take the eyeballs straight out of your head
Say, 'Son, kid, do you want your eyeballs back?'

Did you ever see the people
With the teardrops in their eyes?
Just can't stand it no how
Living in this world of lies

And did you ever hear about the great deception?
Well, the plastic revolutionaries take the money and run
Have you ever been down to Love City
Where they rob you with a smile
Instead of a gun?
Have you ever heard about
The great deception?

Bulbs

I'm kicking off from centrefield
A question of being down for the game
The one-shot deal don't matter
And the other one's the same

Oh my friend, I see you
Want you to come through
And they're standing in the shadows
Where the street lights all turn blue

She's leaving Pan-American
Suitcase in her hand
I said her brothers and her sisters
Are all on Atlantic sand

She's screaming through the alleyway
I hear the lonely cry, why can't you?
And her batteries are corroded
And her hundred-watt bulb just blew

La da da da da, da da da da da
La da da da da, da da da da da

She used to hang out down at Miss Lucy's
Every weekend they would get loose
Now Ada was a straight clear case of
Havin' taken in too much juice

It was outside, and it was outside
Just the nature of the person
Now all you got to remember
After all, it's all show biz

La da da da da, da da da da da
La da da da da, da da da da da

We're just screaming through the alleyway
I hear the lonely cry, ah why can't you?
And they're standing in the shadows
Canal Street lights all turn blue

And they're standing in the shadows
Where the street lights all turn blue
And they're standing in the shadows
Down where the street lights all turn blue

Comfort You

I wanna comfort you
I wanna comfort you
I wanna comfort you

Just let your tears run wild
Like when you were a child
I'll do what I can do
I wanna comfort you

You put the weight on me
You put the weight on me
You put the weight on me

When it gets too much for me
When it gets too much, much too much for me
I'll do the same thing that you do
And I'll put the weight on you

I'll put the weight on you
I'll put the weight on you
And I'll do the same thing that you do
I'll put the weight on you

I wanna comfort you
I wanna comfort you
And I wanna comfort you

Just let your tears run wild
Like when you were a child
I'll do what I can do
I just wanna comfort you

Come Here My Love

Come here, my love
This feeling has me spellbound
It's a storyline, in paragraphs laid down in song
In fathoms of my inner mind
I'm mystified, oh, by this mood
This melancholy feeling that just don't do no good

Come here, my love
And I will lift my spirits high for you
I'd like to fly away and spend a day or two
Just contemplating fields and leaves and talking about
    nothing
Just layin' down in shades of effervescent, effervescent odours
And shades of time and tide
And flowing through
Become enraptured by the sights and sounds and intrigue of
    nature's beauty
Come along with me
And take it all in
Come here, my love

Cul-de-Sac

In the cul-de-sac
Soft, clean eiderdown
Lay you down awhile
And take your rest

It's been much too long
Since you drifted into song
Relax yourself
And hide away

A trifle far
Nearest star
Mount Palomar
And we don't care who you know
It's what you are and who you are

And when they all go home
Down the cobblestones
You can double back
To a cul-de-sac
You can double back
To a cul-de-sac
You can double back
To a cul-de-sac

It Fills You Up

There's something going on
It fill you up, it fill you up, it fill you up now
There's something going on
It fill you up, it fill you up, it fill you up now

But you don't know what it is
But you don't know what it is
But you don't have to know
You just take it for what it is

Within this melody
It fill you up, it fill you up, it fill you up now
There's more than you can see
It fill you up, it fill you up, it fill you up now

There's another realm
There's another world
With kings and queens

That's why you got to testify
It fill you up, it fill you up, it fill you up now
You gotta do and die
It fill you up, it fill you up, it fill you up now

You got to stay on the music and move
You got to turn on the music and groove
Every, every, every day

You know what I'm talking about
It fill you up, it fill you up

It fill you up, it fill you up, it fill you up now
It fill you up, it fill you up, it fill you up now
It fill you up, it fill you up, it fill you up now
Get you rolling in the morning
It fill you up, it fill you up, it fill you up now
Work out a few kinks
It fill you up, it fill you up, it fill you up now
It fill you up to the brim, Jim
It fill you up, it fill you up, it fill you up now
Lord have mercy
It fill you up, it fill you up, it fill you up now
It fill you up, it fill you up, it fill you up now
Come here, baby
It fill you up, it fill you up, it fill you up now

Cold Wind in August

I waited for you
You waited for me
Well, it seemed like
Seemed like a mighty long time

Baby, I had to have you
You know I had to have you
Come rain, rain or shine
It was a cold wind in August
Shivers up and down my spine
I would stand in your garden
In the California pine

I was standin' shiverin'
I got the fever in the rain
But I kept coming back to see you
Again and again and again

I said I had to have you
Baby, I had to have you
Come rain, come rain or shine
It was a cold wind in August
Shivers up and down my spine
I would stand in your garden
In the California pine, California pine

It was a cold wind in August
Shivers up and down my spine
I would stand in your garden
In the California pine, in the California pine

It was a cold wind in August
I was pushed on through September
And I was pushin' through September in the rain
Pushin' through, pushin' through September in the rain

It was a cold wind in August
Shivers up and down my spine
I would stand, stand in your garden
In the California pine

Kingdom Hall

So glad to see you
So glad you're here
Come here beside me now
We can clear inhibition away
All inhibitions
Throw them away
And when we dance like this
We will dance like we've never before

Oh they were swingin'
Down at the Kingdom Hall
Oh bells were ringin'
Down at the Kingdom Hall
A choir was singin'
Down at the Kingdom Hall
They went
'Hey, liley, liley, liley,
Hey, liley, liley, low'

Good body music
Brings you right here
Free-flowin' motion now
When we're shakin' it out on the floor
Good rockin' music
Down in your shoes
And when we dance like this
Like we've never been dancin' before

They were swingin'
Down at the Kingdom Hall
Oh bells were ringin'

Down at the Kingdom Hall
A choir was singin'
Down at Kingdom Hall
They went
'Hey, liley, liley, liley,
Hey, liley, liley, low'

They were swingin'
Down at the Kingdom Hall
Bells were ringin'
Down at the Kingdom Hall
A choir was singin'
Down at the Kingdom Hall
They went
'Hey, liley, liley, liley,
Hey, liley, liley, low'

They were swingin'
Down at the Kingdom Hall
Oh bells were ringin'
Down at the Kingdom Hall
A choir was singin'
Down at the Kingdom Hall
They all went
'Hey, liley, liley, liley,
Hey, liley, liley, low

'Hey, liley, liley,
Hey, liley, low, low, low'
Down at the Kingdom Hall
Bells were ringin' out
And the choir was singin'
And the choir was singin'
'Hey, liley, liley,
Hey liley low, liley low, liley low,

Do do, do do, do do, do do'
Sugar was tough
Sugar was rough
Did you see Sugar?
Down at the Kingdom Hall
They were havin' a party
They were havin' a ball
And the people were dancin'
Down at the Kingdom Hall
Sugar was tough
Sugar was tough

Wavelength

This is a song about your wavelength
And my wavelength, baby
You turn me on
When you get me on your wavelength now
Yeah, yeah, yeah, yeah, yeah
With your wavelength
Oh with your wavelength
With your wavelength
With your wavelength
Oh mama, oh mama, oh mama
Oh mama, oh mama, oh mama, oh mama

Wavelength
Oh my, my
Wavelength
You never let me down, no, no
You never let me down, no, no

When I'm down you always comfort me
When I'm lonely, child, you see about me
You are everywhere you're supposed to be
And I can get your station
When I need rejuvenation

Wavelength
Oh my, my
Wavelength
You never let me down, no, no
You never let me down, no, no

I heard the Voice of America

Callin' on my wavelength
Tellin' me to tune in on my radio
I heard the Voice of America
Callin' on my wavelength
Singin', 'Come back, baby,
Come back,
Come back, baby
Come back'

Won't you sing that song again for me
About my lover, my lover in the grass?
You have told me 'bout my destiny
Singin', 'Come back, baby,
Come back,
Come back, baby,
Come back'

Wavelength
Oh my, my
Wavelength
You never let me down, no, no
You never let me down, no, no

When you get me on
When you get me on your wavelength
When you get me
Oh yeah, Lord
You get me on your wavelength

You got yourself a boy
When you get me on
Get me on your wavelength
Ya radio, ya radio, ya radio
Ya radio, ya radio, ya radio
Ya radio, ya radio, ya radio
Ya radio, ya radio, ya radio

Bright Side of the Road

From the dark end of the street
To the bright side of the road
We'll be lovers once again
On the bright side of the road

Little darlin', come with me
Won't you help me share my load
From the dark end of the street
To the bright side of the road?

And into this life we're born
Baby, sometimes, sometimes we don't know why
And time seems to go by so fast
In the twinkling of an eye

Let's enjoy it while we can
Won't you help me share my load
From the dark end of the street
To the bright side of the road?

And into this life we're born
Baby, sometimes, sometimes we don't know why
And it seems to go by so fast
In the twinkling of an eye

Let's enjoy it while we can
Help me sing my song
Little darlin', come alone
On the bright side of the road

From the dark end of the street

To the bright side of the road
Little darlin', come along
On the bright side of the road

From the dark end of the street
To the bright side of the road
We'll be lovers once again
On the bright side of the road

So we'll be lovers once again
On the bright side of the road

We'll be lovers once again
On the bright side of the road

Rolling Hills

Among the rolling hills
I'll live my life in Him
Well, I will live my life in Him
Among the rolling hills

And with my wife and child
I'll do no man no ill
Oh I will do no man no ill
Among the rolling hills

De de de de de de de de de
De de de de de de de de

Well, among the rolling hills
I read my Bible still
Oh I will read my Bible still
Among the rolling hills

With my pen I'll write my song
Among the rolling hills
With my pen I'll write my song
Among the rolling hills

De de de de de de de de de
De de de de de de de

And I will do my jig
Among the rolling hills
And I will do my jig and live
Among the rolling hills

With my pen I'll write my song
Among the rolling hills
With my pen I'll write my song
Among the rolling hills

And I'll stand and watch it all
Among the rolling hills
And I will stand and watch it all
Among the rolling hills

De de de de de de de de de
De de de de de

Take out my pen and write my song
Among the rolling hills
Take out my pen and write my song
Among the rolling hills
I'll take out my pen and write my song
Among the rolling hills

And the Healing Has Begun

And we'll walk down the avenue again
And we'll sing all the songs from way back when
And we'll walk down the avenue again
When the healing has begun

And we'll walk down the avenue in style
And we'll walk down the avenue and we'll smile
And we'll say, 'Baby, ain't it all worthwhile'
When the healing has begun

I want you to put on your pretty summer dress
You can wear your Easter bonnet and all the rest
And I wanna make love to you, yes, yes, yes
When the healing has begun
When the healing has begun

When you hear the music ringing in your soul
And you feel it in your heart and it grows and grows
And it came from the backstreet rock 'n' roll
When the healing has begun
That's where you come from, man

I want you to put on your, your old summer red dress
Put on your Easter bonnet and all the rest
And I wanna make love to you, yes, yes
When the healing has begun
I can't stand myself

We're gonna make music underneath the stars
We're gonna play to the violin and the two guitars
And we'll sit there for playing in hours

For hours, and hours, and hours, and hours, and hours
And hours, and hours, and hours
When the healing has begun
And hours, and hours, and hours, and hours
When the, when the healing has begun
Wait a minute

Listen, listen, listen, listen
I didn't know you stayed up so late
Ah you know I just got home from a, from a gig
I saw you standing on the street
Just let me move on up here
There's a windowsill a little bit here
Yeah, as I got some, dig some sherry, a drop of port
Yeah, I want you to come on in behind
Behind this door here
Why don't you just move on up this letterbox?
Why don't we just go in your front room and
Just sit down on the settee?
I'll just move on a little, a little bit now
Yeah, I gotta play this Muddy Waters record you got here
If you just open up a little bit there and just let me
Come on in, you know some backstreet jelly roll

We're gonna stay out all night long
And then we're gonna go out and roam across the fields
Baby, you know how I feel
When the healing has begun
When the healing, when the healing has begun
When the healing, when the healing has begun
We're gonna dance, we're gonna stay out all night long
We're gonna dance to the rock 'n' roll
When the healing has begun
Oh baby, now you just let me ease on a little bit
Dig this backstreet jelly roll

And the healing, and the healing has begun
And the healing has begun
And the healing, and the healing

You Know What They're Writing About

You know
You, you know what they're writing about
Baby, you, you know what they're talking about
Baby, you, you know what they're writing about
Baby, you know, you know what they're talking about

It's a thing called love
Down through the ages
It makes you wanna cry sometime
It makes you feel like you wanna lay down and die sometime
It make you high sometime
But when you really get in, in, in, in
It lifts you right up
You know what
You know what
You know what they're talking about
Baby, you, you, you, you, you, you, you, you, you know what
What they're writing about

It's a thing
It's a thing
It's love, baby

Ain't it a wonderful game?
Ain't it a wonderful, a marvellous game?

Ain't it a wonderful, ain't it a wonderful
Ain't it a wonderful game?
Yeah, when there's no more words to say about love, about
    love
It's all in the game, you know what they're talking about

Meet me down, meet me down
Meet me down by the river, baby
Meet me down, meet me down by the river

Meet me down, meet me down
Meet me by, by the water
Meet me down by the water
Baby, you know, I said you know what they're
You know what they're talking about

I want you to meet me, meet me down by the pylons
Meet me down by the pylons, meet me down by the pylons
Meet me down by the pylons

Meet me, I said meet me
I've got something I want to give to you
I've got something I want to give you
I want you to meet me
I want you to meet me
I want you to meet me

Are you there, I want you to meet me
Are you there, I want you to meet me
Are you there, are you there?
And you're there, and you're there
I want you to meet me
And no, no, no, no, no, no
And no, no, no
And no
And no, and no, no
And no
And no
I want you to meet
Are you, are you there?
I want you to be

Are you there?
I want you to meet me
Are you
Are you there, I want you to meet me
There
Are you there?
I want you to meet
Are you there, I want you to meet me
Are you there?
And no, no, no
And no, and no, and no
Are you there?
I want you to meet me

Summertime in England

Will you meet me in the country
In the summertime in England?
Will you meet me
Will you meet me in the country
In the summertime in England?
Will you meet me?
We'll go riding up to Kendal in the country
In the summertime in England
Did you ever hear about
Did you ever hear about
Did you ever hear about Wordsworth and Coleridge?
Did you ever hear about Wordsworth and Coleridge?
They were smokin' up in Kendal
By the lakeside

Can you meet me in the country in the long grass
In the summertime in England?
Will you meet me
With your red robe dangling all around your body
With your red robe dangling all around your body?
Will you meet me?
Did you ever hear about, did you ever hear about
Did you ever hear about, did you ever hear about
Did you ever hear about, did you ever hear about
William Blake
T. S. Eliot
In the summer
In the countryside?
They were smokin'
Summertime in England

Won't you meet me down by Bristol
Meet me along by Bristol?
We'll go riding down
Down by Avalon
Down by Avalon
Down by Avalon
In the countryside in England
With your red robe dangling, with your red robe dangling all
    around your body free
Let your red robe go
Go ridin' down by Avalon
Would you meet me in the country
In the summertime in England?
Would you meet me
In the church of St John
In the church of St John
In the church of St John
Down by Avalon
Down by Avalon
Down by Avalon
Down by Avalon?

Holy magnet
Give you attraction
I was attracted to you
Your coat was old, ragged and worn
And you wore it down through the ages
Ah the sufferin' did show in your eyes as we spoke
And the gospel music
The voice of Mahalia Jackson came through the ether

Oh my common one with the coat so old
And the light in the head
Said, Daddy, don't stroke me
Call me the common one

I said, oh the common one, my illuminated one
Oh my high-in-the-art-of-sufferin' one
Take a walk with me, take a walk with me down by Avalon
Oh my common one with the coat so old
And the light in the head
Keep the sufferin' so fine, and the sufferin' so fine
Take a walk with me down, down by Avalon
And I will show you it ain't why, why, why
It ain't why, why, why
It ain't why, why, why
It just is

Will you meet me in the country?
Will you meet me in the long grass down the country in the
    summertime?
Can you meet me in the long grass?
Wait a minute

With your red robe, with your red robe danglin'
All around your body
Yeats and Lady Gregory corresponded, corresponded
Corresponded, corresponded
And James Joyce wrote streams-of-consciousness books
Streams of
T. S. Eliot chose England, T. S. Eliot chose England
T. S. Eliot joined the ministry, joined the ministry, joined the
    ministry

Did you ever hear about, did you ever hear about
Wordsworth and Coleridge
Smokin' up in Kendal?
They were smokin' by the lakeside
Let your red robe go, let your red robe go
Let your red robe dangle in the countryside in England

We'll go ridin' down by Avalon in the country in the
    summertime in England
With you by my side
Let your red robe go, let your red robe go
You'll be happy dancin'
You'll be happy dancin'
You'll be happy dancin' in your red robe
Let it go, let it go, let it go, let your red robe go

Won't you meet me down by Avalon
In the summertime in England
In the church of St John
In the church of St John
In the church of St John
In the church of St John
In the church of St John?

Did you ever hear about Jesus walkin'
Jesus walkin' down by Avalon?
Can you feel the light in England?
Can you feel the light in England?
Can you feel the light in England?
Can you feel the light in England?

Oh my common one with the light in the head
And the coat so old
And the sufferin' so fine
Take a walk with me
Oh my common one, oh my illuminated one
Down by Avalon, down by Avalon
Oh my common one, oh my illuminated one
Oh my story time one
Oh my treasury in the sunset
Take a walk with me and I will show you

It ain't why, why, why, why
Why, why, why, why, why
Why, why, why, why, why
Why, why, why, why, why, why
It ain't why
It just is

It ain't why, why, why, why
Why, why, why, why, why
Why, why, why, why
It ain't why, why, why
It just is

It ain't why, why, why, why
Why, why, why
It just is

Oh my common one with the light in the head
And the coat so old
Oh my high-in-the-art-of-sufferin' one
Oh my high, oh my high, oh my high-in-the-art-of-sufferin' one
Oh my high-in-the-art-of-sufferin' one

Oh, my common one
Take a walk with me down by Avalon
And I will show you it ain't
It ain't why, why, why
It ain't why, why, why, why
It ain't why, it ain't why
It just is

Oh my common one with the light in the head
And the coat so fine
And the sufferin' is so high
Alright now

[89]

Oh my common one
Oh my common one
Oh my common one
Oh my common one
With the sufferin' so fine

It ain't why, why
It ain't why, why, why
It ain't why, why
It ain't why
It just is, that's all
It just is, that's all

Oh, oh my common one
With the coat so old and the light in the head
And the sufferin' and the sufferin' so fine
And the sufferin' so high

It ain't why
It ain't why
It ain't why
No, it ain't why
It just is, that's all about it
It just is
It just is, that's all there is to it
It just is, that's all there is about it
It just is, that's all there is to it
It just is, it just is

It just is right now
I want to go to church right now and say it just is
It just is, it just is

Oh my common one, my lovely headed one
Oh my high, oh my high-in-the-art-of-sufferin' one

It ain't why, why
It just is, that's all there is about it
Take a walk with me, talk with me
I will show you
It ain't why, it ain't why
It just is

Can you feel the light
Can you feel the light
Can you feel the light
Can you feel the light
Can you feel the light
Can you feel the light
Can you feel the light
Can you feel the light in your soul
In your soul, in your soul, in your soul, in your soul?
Ain't it high
Ain't it high
Ain't it high now

Oh my common one
Oh my story-time one
Oh my high-in-the-art-of-sufferin' one
Put your head on my shoulder
Put your head on my shoulder
And you listen, and you listen to the silence
Can you feel the silence?
Can you feel the silence?

Celtic Ray

When Llewellyn comes around
And he goes through market town
You'll be on the Celtic Ray
Are you ready?

When McManus comes around
On his early-morning round
Crying, 'Herring olay'
You'll be on the Celtic Ray

Ireland, Scotland, Brittany and Wales
I can hear those mothers' voices calling
'Children, children, children'

When the coal-brick man comes round
On a cold November day
You'll be on the Celtic Ray
Are you ready, are you ready?

Ireland, Scotland, Brittany and Wales
I can hear those mothers' voices calling
'Children, children, children'

Listen, Jimmy, I wanna go home
Listen, Jimmy, I wanna go home
I've been away from the Ray too long
I've been away from the Ray too long

All over Ireland, Scotland, Brittany and Wales
I can hear the mothers' voices calling
'Children, children, come home, children

Children, come home on the Celtic Ray'

In the early morning we'll go walkin'
Where the light comes shining through
On the Celtic Ray
Come on, children, come on, the Celtic Ray

Dweller on the Threshold
(Van Morrison and Hugh Murphy)

I'm a dweller on the threshold
And I'm waiting at the door
And I'm standing in the darkness
I don't want to wait no more

I have seen without perceiving
I have been another man
Let me pierce the realm of glamour
So I know just what I am

I'm a dweller on the threshold
And I'm waiting at the door
And I'm standing in the darkness
I don't want to wait no more

Feel the angel of the present
In the mighty crystal fire
Lift me up, consume my darkness
Let me travel even higher

I'm a dweller on the threshold
As I cross the burning ground
Let me go down to the water
Watch the great illusion drown

I'm a dweller on the threshold
And I'm waiting at the door
And I'm standing in the darkness
I don't want to wait no more

I'm gonna turn and face the music

The music of the spheres
Lift me up, consume my darkness
When the midnight disappears

I will walk out of the darkness
And I'll walk into the light
And I'll sing the song of ages
And the dawn will end the night

I'm a dweller on the threshold
And I'm waiting at the door
And I'm standing in the darkness
I don't want to wait no more

I'm a dweller on the threshold
And I cross the burning ground
And I'll go down to the water
Let the great illusion drown

I'm a dweller on the threshold
And I'm waiting at the door
And I'm standing in the darkness
I don't want to wait no more

I'm a dweller on the threshold
Dweller on the threshold
I'm a dweller on the threshold
I'm a dweller on the threshold

Beautiful Vision

Beautiful vision
Stay with me all of the time
Beautiful vision
Stay ever on my mind with your beautiful vision

Mystical rapture
I am in ecstasy
Beautiful vision
Don't ever separate me with your beautiful vision

In the darkest night
You are shining bright
You are my guiding light
You show me wrong from right

Beautiful vision
Stay ever on my mind
Beautiful vision
Stay with me all of the time with your beautiful vision

In the darkest night
You are shining bright
You are my guiding light
Show me wrong from right

Beautiful vision
Stay with me all of the time
Beautiful vision
Stay ever on my mind with your beautiful vision

I can make it
I can make it
With your beautiful vision

She Gives Me Religion

Down the mystic avenue I walk again
Remembering the days gone by
And I'm knocking with my heart
And all the girls walk by
In all their summer fashion
And the church bells chime
On a summer Sunday afternoon

She gives me religion
She gives me religion

And the angel of imagination
Opened up my gate
She said, 'Come right in,
I saw you knocking with your heart'

And the angel of imagination
Said, 'Lift your fiery vision bright,
Let your flame burn into the night,
I saw you knocking with your heart'

She gives me religion
She gives me religion

And all the girls walk by
In all their summer fashion
And the church bells chime
On a summer Sunday afternoon

She gives me religion
I said she gives me religion

And I'm knocking
And I'm knocking with my heart
And I'm knocking
Knocking with my heart
And I'm knocking with my heart

Cleaning Windows

Oh the smell of the bakery from across the street
Got in my nose
As we carried our ladders down the street
With the wrought-iron gate rows
I went home and listened to Jimmie Rodgers in my lunch
    break
Bought five Woodbine at the shop on the corner
And went straight back to work

Oh Sam was up on top
And I was on the bottom with the V
We went for lemonade and Paris buns
At the shop and broke for tea
I collected from the lady
And I cleaned the fanlight inside out
I was blowing saxophone on the weekend
In a Down joint

What's my line?
I'm happy cleaning windows
Take my time, I'll see you when my love grows
Baby, don't let it slide, I'm a working man in my prime
Cleaning windows
Number 36!

I heard Leadbelly and Blind Lemon
On the street where I was born
Sonny Terry, Brownie McGhee and
Muddy Waters singin' 'I'm a Rollin' Stone'
I went home and read my Christmas Humphreys book on
    Zen

Curiosity Killed the Cat
Kerouac's *Dharma Bums* and *On the Road*

What's my line?
I'm happy cleaning windows
Take my time, I'll see you when my love grows
Baby, don't let it slide, I'm a working man in my prime
Cleaning windows

What's my line?
I'm happy cleaning windows
Well, I take my time, I'll see you when my love grows
Don't let it slide, I'm a working man in my prime
Cleaning windows

Cleaning, what you sayin', number, number 126
Aye, we'll be round tomorrow
I just found a tanner and a 3d bit on the windowsill here
C'mon, Sammy, hurry up
If we don't get finished we'll have to go down to the dole
Cleaning windows

Higher Than the World

Well, I'm higher
Than the world
And I'm livin'
In my dreams
I'll make it better than it seems today

And I'm higher
Than a cloud
And I'm livin'
In a sound
I'll make it better than it seems today

Higher than the world
But my head is in a swirl
I got to give life a whirl today

Higher than the clouds
Wrapped up in a sound
I make it better all around today

Higher than the world
And my head is in a swirl
I got to give life a whirl today

Higher in my mind
I'm gonna leave these blues behind
And I'll find what I'll find today

'Cause I'm higher than the world
And I'm wrapped up in my dreams
I'll make it better than it seems today

Yes, I'm higher than the world
And I'm livin' in my mind
I got to hold on to what I find today
Just a little bit higher

River of Time

Heart and soul
Body and mind
Heart and soul
Body and mind
Heart and soul
Body and mind
Meet me on the river of time
Meet me on the river of time

Brother of mine
Sister of mine
Brother of mine
Sister of mine
Heart and soul
Body and mind
Meet me on the river of time
Meet me on the river of time

Lover of soul
Lover of mine
Lover of soul
Lover of mine
Heart and soul
Body and mind
Meet me on the river of time
Meet me on the river of time
Meet me on the river of time
On the river
River of time
On the river of time
On the river of time

Cry for Home

I'll be waiting
I'll be waiting on that shore
To hear the cry for home
You won't have to worry any more
When you hear the cry for home

When you hear, hear the call
You won't have to think at all
Hear the cry for home

I'll be standing
I'll be standing within reach
When you hear, hear the call
I'll be waiting
I'll be waiting in the breach
For you, when you hear

When you hear, hear the call
You won't have to think at all
Hear the cry for home

When I listen
When I listen to the song
Well, it feels, feels so free
And you tell me
You will come and go with me
When you hear the cry for home

When you hear, hear the call
You won't have to think at all
Hear the cry for home

When you hear, hear the call
You won't have to think at all
Hear the cry for home

When you hear, hear the call
You won't have to think at all
Hear the cry for home

Rave on, John Donne/Rave on, Part Two

Rave on, John Donne, rave on, thy holy fool
Down through the weeks of ages
In the moss-borne dark dank pools

Rave on down through the Industrial Revolution
Empiricism, the atomic and nuclear age
Rave on down through the corridors
Rave on words on printed page

Rave on, Walt Whitman, nose down in wet grass
Rave on, fill the senses
On nature's bright-green shady path

Rave on, Omar Khayyam, rave on, Khalil Gibran
Oh what sweet wine we drinketh
The celebration will be held
We will drink the wine and break the holy bread

Rave on, let a man come out of Ireland
Rave on, Mr Yeats, rave on down through thy holy Rosy Cross
Rave on down through Theosophy and the Golden Dawn
Rave on through the writing of *A Vision*
Rave on, rave on, rave on, rave on, rave on, rave on, rave on

Rave on, John Donne, rave on, thy holy fool
Down through the weeks of ages
In the moss-borne dark dank pools

Rave on down through the Industrial Revolution
Empiricism, and the atomic and nuclear age
Rave on words on printed page

Tonight 'neath the silvery moon, tonight
Tonight 'neath the silvery moon, tonight
And the leaves shake out of the trees
And the cool summer breeze
And the people passing in the street
And everybody that you meet

Tonight you will understand the oneness
Tonight you will understand the one
Tonight 'neath the silvery moon, tonight
Tonight, let it all begin, tonight
You will understand the oneness
The oneness, the oneness, the oneness, the oneness
The oneness, the oneness, the oneness

You made it real, what you sang about in your song
You made it real, what you sang about in your song
I said, 'Come back, baby, can we talk it over
One more time, tonight?'

Tonight you will understand the one, the oneness
Tonight 'neath the silvery moon, tonight
Tonight, let it all begin, tonight
You will understand the oneness
The oneness, the oneness, the oneness

And the truth what you sang about in your song
Oh baby, baby
And the truth what you sang about in your song
I said, 'No, no, no, no, no, no, no, no, no
No, no, no, no, no, no, no, no, no, no
No, no, no, no, no, no, no, no, no, no'

Tonight you will understand the one
Oh tonight you will under, understand the oneness

And the leaves shakin' on the trees
In the cool evening breeze
And the people passing in the street
And everybody that you meet
Tonight, tonight
When your lover's gone
Tonight, tonight

*

Tonight 'neath the silvery moon, tonight
Tonight 'neath the silvery moon, tonight
And the leaves shake out of the trees
And the cool summer breeze
And the people passing in the street
And everybody that you meet

Tonight you will understand the oneness
Tonight you will understand the one
Tonight 'neath the silvery moon, tonight
Tonight, let it all begin, tonight
You will understand the oneness
The oneness, the oneness, the oneness, the oneness
The oneness, the oneness, the oneness

You made it real, what you sang about in your song
You made it real, what you sang about in your song
I said, 'Come back, baby, can we talk it over
One more time, tonight?'

Tonight you will understand the one, the oneness
Tonight 'neath the silvery moon, tonight
Tonight, let it all begin, tonight
You will understand the oneness
The oneness, the oneness, the oneness

And the truth what you sang about in your song
Oh baby, baby
And the truth what you sang about in your song
I said, 'No, no, no, no, no, no, no, no, no
No, no, no, no, no, no, no, no, no, no
No, no, no, no, no, no, no, no, no, no'

Tonight you will understand the one
Oh tonight you will under, understand the oneness
And the leaves shakin' on the trees
In the cool evening breeze
And the people passing in the street
And everybody that you meet
Tonight, tonight
When your lover's gone
Tonight, tonight

Tore Down à la Rimbaud

Showed me pictures in the gallery
Showed me novels on the shelf
Put my hands across the table
Gave me knowledge of myself

Showed me visions, showed me nightmares
Gave me dreams that never end
Showed me light out of the tunnel
When there was darkness all around instead

I was just tore down à la Rimbaud
And I wish my message would come
Tore down à la Rimbaud
You know it's hard sometime
You know it's hard sometime

Showed me ways and means and motions
Showed me what it's like to be
Gave me days of deep devotion
Showed me things that I cannot see

Well, I was tore down à la Rimbaud
And I wish my purpose would come
Tore down à la Rimbaud
You know it's hard sometime
You know it's hard sometime

Showed me different shapes and colours
Showed me many different roads
Gave me very clear instructions
When I was in the dark night of the soul

When I was tore down à la Rimbaud
And I wish my writing would come
Tore down à la Rimbaud
You know it's hard sometime
You know it's hard sometime

Tore down à la Rimbaud
And I wish my writing would come
Tore down à la Rimbaud
You know it's hard sometime
You know it's hard sometime

Hard sometime
Tore down à la Rimbaud, à la Rimbaud
I was tore down à la Rimbaud, à la Rimbaud

Got to Go Back

When I was a young boy back in Orangefield
I used to look out my classroom window and dream
And then go home and listen to Ray sing
'I Believe to My Soul' after school
Ah that love that was within me
You know it carried me through
And it lifted me up and it filled me
Meditation, contemplation too

Got to go back
We've got to go back
Got to go back
Got to go back
For the healing
Go on with the dreaming

Ah there's people in the street
And the summer's almost here
Got to go outside in the fresh air
And walk while it's still clear
Breathe it in all the way down
To your stomach too
Breathe it out with a radiance
Into the night-time air

Got to go back
We've got to go back
Got to go back
Got to go back
For the healing
Go on with the dreaming

Got my ticket at the airport
Well, guess I've been marking time
I've been living in another country
That operates along entirely different lines
Keep me away from port or whiskey
Don't play anything sentimental it'll make me cry
Got to go now, my friend
Is there really any need to ask why?

Got to go back
Got to go back
Got to go back
We've got to go back
For the healing
Go on with the dreaming

We've got to go back
Baby, we've got to go back
Got to go back
Got to go back
For the healing
Go on with the dreaming

With the dreaming
With the dreaming
With the dreaming

In the Garden

The fields are always wet with rain
After a summer shower
When I saw you standing, standing in the garden
In the garden wet with rain

You wiped the teardrops from your eye in sorrow
As we watched the petals fall down to the ground
And as I sat beside you
I felt the great sadness that day
In the garden

And then one day you came back home
You were a creature all in rapture
You had the key to your soul and you did open
That day you came back
To the garden

The olden summer breeze was blowin' against your face
The light of God was shinin' on your countenance divine
And you were a violet colour
As you sat beside your father and your mother
In the garden

The summer breeze was blowin' on your face
Within your violet you treasure your summery words
And as the shiver from my neck down to my spine
Ignited me in daylight and nature
In the garden

And you went into a trance
Your childlike vision became so fine

And we heard the bells within the church we loved so much
And felt the presence of the youth of eternal summers
In the garden

And as it touched your cheeks so lightly
Born again you were and blushed
And we touched each other lightly
And we felt the presence of the Christ within our hearts
In the garden

And I turned to you and I said
'No guru, no method, no teacher,
Just you and I and nature and the Father
In the garden

'No guru, no method, no teacher,
Just you and I and nature
And the Father and the Son and the Holy Ghost
In the garden wet with rain

'No guru, no method, no teacher,
Just you and I and nature
And the Father and the Son and the Holy Ghost
In the garden,
In the garden wet with rain

'No guru, no method, no teacher,
Just you and I and nature and the Father
In the garden'

One Irish Rover

Tell me the story now
Now that it's over
Wrap it in glory
For one Irish Rover

Tell me you're wiser now
Tell me you're older
Wrap it in glory
For one Irish Rover

I can tell by the light in your eye
That you're so far away
Like a ship out on the sea without a sail
You've gone astray

Tell me the facts real straight
Don't make me over
Wrap it in glory
For one Irish Rover

Tell me you've seen the light
Tell me you know me
Make it come out alright
And wrap it in glory

For one Irish Rover
For one Irish Rover
For one Irish Rover
For one Irish Rover

Foreign Window

I saw you from a foreign window
Bearing down the suffering road
You were carrying your burden
To the palace of the Lord
To the palace of the Lord

I spied you from a foreign window
When the lilacs were in bloom
And the sun shone through your windowpane
To the place you kept your books
You were reading on your sofa
You were singing every prayer
That the masters had instilled in you
Since Lord Byron loved despair
In the palace of the Lord

And if you don't get it right this time
You don't have to come back again
And if you get it right this time
There's no need to explain

I saw you from a foreign window
Bearing down the suffering road
You were carrying your burden
You were singing about Rimbaud
I was going down to Geneva
When the kingdom had been found
I was giving you protection
From the loneliness of the crowd
In the palace of the Lord

They were giving you religion
Breaking bread and drinking wine
And you laid out on the green hills
Just like when you were a child
I saw you from a foreign window
You were trying to find your way back home
You were carrying your defects
Sleeping on a pallet on the floor
In the palace of the Lord
In the palace of the Lord
In the palace of the Lord

Tir Na Nog

We were standing in the kingdom
And by the mansion gate
We stood enraptured by the silence
As the birds sang their heavenly song
In Tir Na Nog

We stopped in the Church of Ireland
And prayed to Our Father
And climbed up the mountainside
With fire in our hearts
And we walked all the
Way to Tir Na Nog

I said with my eyes that
I recognised your chin
It was my long-lost friend
To help me from another lifetime
We took each other's hand and cried
Like a river when we said hello
And we walked all the way to Tir Na Nog

We made a big connection
On a golden autumn day
We were standing in the
Garden wet with rain
And our souls were young again
In Tir Na Nog

And outside the storm was raging
Outside Jerusalem
We drove in our chariots of fire

Following the sun in the west
Going up, going up to
Tir Na Nog

You came into my life
And you filled me and you filled me
Oh so joyous by the clear cool crystal streams
Where the roads were quiet and still
And we walked all the way
To Tir Na Nog

How can we not be attached?
After all we're only human
The only way then is to never come back
Except I wouldn't want that, would you
If we weren't together again
In Tir Na Nog

We've been together before
In a different incarnation
And we loved each other
Then as well
And we sat down in contemplation
Many, many, many times
You kissed mine eyes
In Tir Na Nog

I Forgot that Love Existed

I forgot that love existed, trouble in my mind
Heartache after heartache, worried all the time
I forgot that love existed
Then I saw the light
Everyone around me made everything alright

Oh Socrates and Plato
They praised it to the skies
Everyone who's ever loved
Everyone who's ever tried

If my heart could do the thinkin'
And my head begin to feel
Well, I'll look upon the world anew
And know what's truly real

Well, I forgot that love existed
And it strangled up my heart
Then I turned a brand-new leaf
And made a brand-new start

If my heart could do my thinkin'
And my head begin to feel
Well, I'd look upon the world anew
And know what's truly real

What's truly real
I forgot that love existed
And now it's alright
I forgot that love existed
And now it's alright

Someone Like You

I've been searching a long time
For someone exactly like you
I've been travelling all around the world
Waiting for you to come through
Someone like you; make it all worthwhile
Someone like you; keep me satisfied
Someone exactly like you

I've been travelling a hard road
Looking for someone exactly like you
I've been carrying my heavy load
Waiting for the light to come shining through
Someone like you; make it all worthwhile
Someone like you; make me satisfied
Someone exactly like you

I've been doing some soul-searching
To find out where you're at
I've been up and down the highway
In all kinds of foreign lands
Someone like you; make it all worthwhile
Someone like you; keep me satisfied
Someone exactly like you

I've been all around the world
Marching to the beat of a different drum
But just lately I have realised
The best is yet to come
Someone like you; make it all worthwhile
Someone like you; keep me satisfied
Someone exactly like you

Someone exactly like you
Someone exactly like you
The best is yet to come
The best is yet to come
Someone exactly like you

Alan Watts Blues

Well, I'm taking some time with my quiet friend
Well, I'm taking some time on my own
Well, I'm making some plans for my getaway
There'll be blue skies shining way up above

When I'm cloud-hidden
When I'm cloud-hidden
When I'm cloud-hidden
Whereabouts unknown

Well, I have to get out of the rat race now
Well, I'm tired of the ways of mice and men
And the empires are all turning into rust again
Out of everything nothing remains the same

That's why I'm cloud-hidden
Why I'm cloud-hidden
That's why I'm cloud-hidden
Whereabouts unknown

Sitting up on the mountain top
In my solitude
Where the fog comes rolling in
Just might do me some good

Well, I'm waiting in the clearing, with my motor on
Well, it's time to get back to the town again
Where the air is sweet and fresh in the countryside
Well, it won't be long before, be back here again

When I'm cloud-hidden

I'm cloud-hidden
When I'm cloud-hidden
Whereabouts unknown

I'm cloud-hidden
I'm cloud-hidden
When I'm cloud-hidden
Whereabouts unknown
Whereabouts unknown

Cloud-hidden
Cloud-hidden
Cloud-hidden
Whereabouts unknown

Did Ye Get Healed?

I wanna know did you get the feeling
Did you get it down in your soul?
I wanna know did you get the feeling
And did the feeling grow?

Sometimes when the spirit moves me
I can do many wondrous things
I wanna know when the spirit moves you
Did you get healed?

When I begin to realise it manifest in my life
In oh so many ways
Every day I wanna talk about it and walk about it
Every day I wanna be closer

I wanna know did you get the feeling?
Did you get it down in your soul?
I wanna know did you get the feeling?
Oh did you get healed?

When I begin to realise the magic in my life
See it manifest in oh so many ways
Every day it's getting better and better
I wanna be daily walking, daily walking close

It gets stronger when you get the feeling
When you get it down in your soul
And it make you feel good
And it make you feel whole

When the spirit moves you

And it fills you through and through
Every morning and at the break of day
Did you get healed?

Did you get healed?
Did you get healed?

Irish Heartbeat

Oh won't you stay, stay awhile
With your own ones?
Don't ever stray
Stray so far from your own ones
For the world is so cold
Don't care nothin' for your soul
You share with your own ones

Don't rush away, rush away
From your own ones
One more day, one more day
With your own ones
This old world is so cold
Don't care nothin' for your soul
You share with your own ones

There's a stranger
And he's standing by your door
Might be your best friend
Might be your brother
You may never know

I'm going back, going back
To my own ones
Back to talk, talk awhile
With my own ones
This old world is so cold
Don't care nothing for your soul
You share with your own ones

This old world is so cold
Don't care nothing for your soul
You share with your own ones

Whenever God Shines His Light

Whenever God shines His light on me
Open up my eyes so I can see
When I look up in the darkest night
I know everything's going to be alright

In deep confusion, in great despair
When I reach out for Him, He is there
When I am lonely as I can be
I know that God shines His light on me

Reach out for Him, He'll be there
With Him your troubles you can share
If you live the life you love
You get the blessing from above

He heals the sick and He heals the lame
Says you can do it too in Jesus's name
He'll lift you up and He turns you around
And puts your feet back on higher ground

Reach out for Him, He'll be there
With Him your troubles you can share
You can use His higher power
Every day and any hour

He heals the sick and He heals the lame
And He says you can heal them too in Jesus's name
He lifts you up and He turns you around
And puts your feet back on higher ground

Where He shines His light
Whenever God shines His light, on you, on you

He is the way, He is the truth, He is the light
Puts your feet back, puts your feet back
On higher ground, puts your feet back
Higher ground

Puts your feet back, puts your feet back
On higher ground, puts your feet back
On higher ground

Have I Told You Lately that I Love You?

Have I told you lately that I love you?
Have I told you there's no one above you?
Fill my heart with gladness
Take away my sadness
Ease my troubles, that's what you do

Oh the morning sun in all its glory
Greets the day with hope and comfort too
And you fill my life with laughter
You can make it better
Ease my troubles, that's what you do

There's a love that's divine
And it's yours and it's mine
Like the sun
At the end of the day
We should give thanks and pray to the One and say

Have I told you lately that I love you?
Have I told you there's no one above you?
Fill my heart with gladness
Take away my sadness
Ease my troubles, that's what you do

There's a love that's divine
And it's yours and it's mine
And it shines like the sun
At the end of the day
We will give thanks and pray to the One

Have I told you lately that I love you?

Have I told you there's no one above you?
Fill my heart with gladness
Take away my sadness
Ease my troubles, that's what you do

Take away my sadness
Fill my life with gladness
Ease my troubles, that's what you do

Fill my life with gladness
Take away my sadness
Ease my troubles, that's what you do

Coney Island

Coming back from Downpatrick
Stopping off at St John's Point
Out all day bird-watching
And the *craic* was good

Stopped off at Strangford Lough
Early in the morning
Drove through Shrigley taking pictures
And on to Killyleagh
Stopping for Sunday papers at the
Lecale district just before Coney Island

On and on, over the hill to Ardglass in the jam jar
Autumn sunshine, magnificent and all shining through
Stop off at Ardglass for a couple of jars of
Mussels and some potted herrings in case
We get famished before dinner

On and on, over the hill, and the *craic* is good
Heading towards Coney Island
I look at the side of your face
As the sunlight comes streaming through the window
In the autumn sunshine
And all the time going to Coney Island I'm thinking
'Wouldn't it be great if it was like this all the time?'

Orangefield

On a golden autumn day
You came my way in Orangefield
Saw you standing by the riverside in Orangefield
How I loved you then in Orangefield
Like I love you now in Orangefield

And the sun shone on your hair
When I saw you there in Orangefield
Saw you standing by the riverside in Orangefield
How I loved you then in Orangefield
Like I love you now in Orangefield

And the sun shone so bright
And it lit up all our days
You were the apple of my eye
Baby, it's true

On a golden autumn day
All my dreams came true in Orangefield
On a throne of Ulster day
You came my way in Orangefield
How I loved you then in Orangefield
Like I love you now in Orangefield

And the sun shone so bright
And it lit up all our lives
And the apple of my eye
Baby, was you

On a throne of Ulster day
You came my way in Orangefield

Saw you standing by the riverside in Orangefield
How I loved you then in Orangefield
Like I love you now in Orangefield

How I loved you then in Orangefield
Like I love you now in Orangefield

These Are the Days

These are the days of the endless summer
These are the days, the time is now
There is no past, there's only future
There's only here, there's only now

Oh your smiling face, your gracious presence
The fires of spring are kindling bright
Oh the radiant heart and the song of glory
Crying freedom in the night

These are the days by the sparkling river
His timely grace and our treasured find
This is the love of the one magician
Turned the water into wine

These are the days of the endless dancing
And the long walks on the summer night
These are the days of the true romancing
When I'm holding you oh so tight

These are the days by the sparkling river
And His timely grace and our treasured find
This is the love of the one great magician
Turned the water into wine

These are the days now that we must savour
And we must enjoy as we can
These are the days that will last for ever
You've got to hold them in your heart

So Quiet in Here

Foghorns blowing in the night
Salt sea air in the morning breeze
Driving cars all along the coastline
This must be what it's all about
Oh this must be what it's all about
This must be what paradise is like
So quiet in here, so peaceful in here
So quiet in here, so peaceful in here

The warm look of radiance on your face
And your heart beating close to mine
And the evening fading in the candle glow
This must be what it's all about
Oh this must be what it's all about
This must be what paradise is like
So quiet in here, so peaceful in here
So quiet in here, so peaceful in here

All my struggling in the world
And so many dreams that don't come true
Step back, put it all away
It don't matter, it don't matter any more
Oh this must be what paradise is like
This must be what paradise is like
It's so quiet in here, so peaceful in here
It's so quiet in here, so peaceful in here

A glass of wine with some friends
Talking into the wee hours of the dawn
Sit back and relax your mind
This must be, this must be, what it's all about

This must be what paradise is like
Oh this must be what paradise is like
So quiet in here, so peaceful in here
So quiet in here, so peaceful in here

Big ships out in the night
And we're floating across the waves
Sailing for some other shore
Where we can be what we wanna be
Oh this must be what paradise is like
This must be what paradise is like
Baby, it's so quiet in here, so peaceful in here
So quiet in here, peaceful in here
So quiet in here, so peaceful in here
So quiet in here, so quiet in here
So peaceful in here, so quiet in here

In the Days Before Rock 'n' Roll
(Van Morrison and Paul Durcan)

Justin, gentler than a man
I am down on my knees
At the wireless knobs
I am down on my knees
At those wireless knobs
Telefunken, Telefunken
And I'm searching for
Luxembourg, Luxembourg
Athlone, Budapest, AFN
Hilversum, Helvetia
In the days before rock 'n' roll

In the days before rock 'n' roll
In the days before rock 'n' roll
When we let, then we bet
On Lester Piggott when we met
We let the goldfish go
In the days before rock 'n' roll

Fats did not come in
Without those wireless knobs
Fats did not come in
Without those wireless knobs
Elvis did not come in
Without those wireless knobs
Nor Fats, nor Elvis
Nor Sonny, nor Lightnin'
Nor Muddy, nor John Lee

In the days before rock 'n' roll
In the days before rock 'n' roll

When we let and we bet
On Lester Piggott, ten to one
And we let the goldfish go
Down the stream
Before rock 'n' roll

We went over the wavebands
To get Luxembourg
Luxembourg and Athlone
AFN Stars of Jazz
Come in, come in, come in, Ray Charles
Come in, the high priest

In the days before rock 'n' roll
In the days before rock 'n' roll
When we let and we bet
On Lester Piggott, ten to one
And we let the goldfish go
And then The Killer came along, The Killer
The Killer, Jerry Lee Lewis
'A Whole Lotta Shakin' Goin' on'
'Great Balls of Fire'
Little Richard

Justin, gentler than a man
Justin, Justin, where is Justin now?
What's Justin doing now?
Just, where is Justin now?
Come aboard

Memories

Memories
All I have is memories
All I have is memories
Memories of you

Now you're gone
They linger on, these memories
All these precious memories
Memories of you

How they linger in the twilight
In the morning in the small hours
Just before dawn

Memories
Of summer days so long ago
People and the places
That we used to know
Oh those memories

How they linger in the twilight
And in the wee small hours
Sometimes just before the dawn

Oh those memories
Oh happy times, those memories
All I have now is memories
Memories of you

Oh memories
Oh those precious memories

All I have is memories
Memories of you

Memories of you
Memories of you
Oh those memories of you
Oh those memories of you
Oh the precious memories of you
Oh memories of you

Why Must I Always Explain?

Have to toe the line, I've got to make the most
Spent all these years going from pillar to post
Now I'm standing on the outside and I'm waitin' in the rain
Tell me why must I always explain?

Bared my soul to the crowd, but oh what the cost
Most of them laughed out loud like nothing's been lost
There were hypocrites and parasites and people that drain
Tell me why must I always explain?

Why, why must I always explain
Over and over, over again?
It's just a job you know and it's not 'Sweet Lorraine'
Tell me why must I always explain?

Well, I get up in the morning and I get my brief
I go out and stare at the world in complete disbelief
It's not righteous indignation that makes me complain
It's the fact that I always have to explain

I can't be everywhere at once, there's always somebody to see
And I never turned out to be the person that you wanted me
  to be
And I tell you who I am time and time and time again
Tell me why must I always explain?

Well, it's out on the highway and it's on with the show
Always telling people things they're too lazy to know
It can make you crazy, it can drive you insane
Tell me why must I always explain?

See Me Through Part II (Just a Closer Walk with Thee)

Just a closer walk with Thee
Grant it, Jesus, if you please
I'll be satisfied as long as I walk, dear Lord, close to Thee

I am weak but Thou art strong
Jesus, keep me from all wrong
I'll be satisfied as long as I walk, dear Lord, close to Thee

See me through days of wine and roses
By and by when the morning comes
Jazz and blues and folk, poetry and jazz
Voice and music, music and no music
Silence and then voice
Music and writing, words
Memories, memories way back
Take me way back, Hyndford Street and Hank Williams
Louis Armstrong, Sidney Bechet on Sunday afternoons in
    winter
Sidney Bechet, Sunday afternoons in winter
And the tuning in of stations in Europe on the wireless
Before, yes, before this was the way it was
More silence, more breathing together
Not rushing, being
Before rock 'n' roll, before television
Previous, previous, previous
See me through, just a closer walk with Thee

Just a closer walk with Thee
Grant it, Jesus, if you please
I'll be satisfied as long as I walk, dear Lord, close to Thee

I am weak but Thou art strong
Jesus, keep me from all wrong
I'll be satisfied as long as I walk, dear Lord, close to Thee

Take Me Back

I've been walking by the river
I've been walking down by the water
I've been walking down by the river

I've been feeling so sad and blue
I've been thinking, I've been thinking, I've been thinking
I've been thinking, I've been thinking, I've been thinking
And there's so much suffering, and it's too much confusion
Too much, too much confusion in the world

Take me back, take me back, take me back
Take me way back, take me way back, take me way back
Take me way back, take me way back, take me way back
Take me way back, take me way back
Take me way, way, way, way, way, way, way back
Help me, help me understand
Take me, do you remember the time, darlin'
When everything made more sense in the world?
Oh I remember, I remember
When life made more sense
Ah take me back, take me back, take me back, take me back
Take me back, take me back, take me back, take me back
Take me back to when the world made more sense
Well, there's too much suffering and confusion
And I'm walking down by the river
Oh let me understand religion

Way back, way back
When you walked in a green field, in a green meadow
Down an avenue of trees
On a, on a golden summer

And the sky was blue
And you didn't have no worries, you didn't have no care
You were walking in a green field
In a meadow, through the buttercups, in the summertime
And you looked way out over, way out
Way out over the city and the water
And it felt so good and it felt so good
And you keep on walking

And the music on the radio and the music on the radio
Has so much soul, has so much soul
And you listen, in the night-time
While we're still and quiet
And you looked out on the water
And the big ships and the big boats
Came on sailing by, by, by, by
And you felt so good, and I felt so good
I felt I wanna blow my harmonica

Take me back there, take me way back
Take me back, take me back, take me back
Take me way, way, way back, way back
To when, when I understood
When I understood the light, when I understood the light
In the golden afternoon, in the golden afternoon
In the golden afternoon, in the golden afternoon
In the golden afternoons when we sat and listened to Sonny
    Boy blow

In the golden afternoon when we sat and let Sonny Boy blow,
    blow his harp

Take me back, take me back, take me back
Take me way, way, way, way, way, way, way
Back when I, when I understood, when I understood

Oh take me way back, when, when, when, when, when,
    when
When, when, when, when, when, when, when
I was walking down the
Walking down the street in the rain
And it didn't matter
'Cause everything felt, everything felt, everything felt
Everything felt, everything felt, everything felt, everything felt
Everything felt, everything felt, everything felt so right

And so good
Everything felt so right, and so good
Everything felt so right, and so good
Everything felt so right, and so good
Everything felt so right, and so good
Everything felt so right, and so good, so good
In the eternal now, in the eternal moment
In the eternal now, in the eternal moment
In the eternal now
Everything felt so good, so good, so good, so good, so good
And so right, so right, so right, just
So good, so right, so right, in the eternal
In the eternal moment, in the eternal moment
In the eternal moment, in the eternal moment
When you lived, when you lived
When you lived in the light
When you lived in the grace
In the grace, in grace
When you lived in the light
In the light, in the grace
And the blessing

All Saints Day

Here comes Sue and she looks crazy
Skipping down the hillside daily
Looking like the flowers that bloom in May
Won't you make your reservation?
I will meet you at the station
Won't you come and see me, All Saints Day?

Follow the lead, it is no wonder, I seem to be so high
Living my dreams the way I ought to
As the days go rolling by

See me strolling through the meadow
With you, baby, by my side
Won't you come and see me, All Saints Day?

See the streamline blue horizon
With you, baby, by the way
Won't you come and see me, All Saints Day?
You can make your reservation
I will meet you at the station
When you come to see me, All Saints Day

When you come to see me, All Saints Day
When you come to see me, All Saints Day

Hymns to the Silence

Oh my dear, oh my dear sweet love
Oh my dear, oh my dear sweet love
When I'm away from you, when I'm away from you
Well, I feel, well, I feel so sad and blue
Well, I feel, well, I feel so sad and blue
Oh my dear, oh my dear, oh my dear sweet love
When I'm away from you, I just have to sing my hymns
Hymns to the silence, hymns to the silence
Hymns to the silence, hymns to the silence

Oh my dear, oh my dear sweet love, it's a long, long journey
Long, long journey, journey back home
Back home to you, feel you by my side
Long journey, journey, journey
In the midnight, in the midnight, I burn the candle
Burn the candle at both ends, burn the candle at both ends
Burn the candle at both ends, burn the candle at both ends
And I keep on, 'cause I can't sleep at night
Until the daylight comes through
And I just, and I just have to sing, sing my
Hymns to the silence, hymns to the silence
Hymns to the silence, my hymns to the silence

I wanna go out in the countryside
Oh sit by the clear cool crystal water
Get my spirit, way back to the feeling
Deep in my soul, I wanna feel
Oh so close to the one, close to the one
Close to the one, close to the one
And that's why I keep on singing, baby
My hymns to the silence, hymns to the silence

Oh my hymns to the silence, hymns to the silence
Oh hymns to the silence, oh hymns to the silence
Oh hymns to the silence, hymns to the silence
Oh my dear, my dear sweet love
Can you feel the silence, can you feel the silence?
Can you feel the silence, can you feel the silence?

Hymns to the silence, hymns to the silence
Hymns to the silence, hymns to the silence
Hymns to the silence, hymns to the silence
Hymns to the silence, hymns to the silence
Hymns to the silence, hymns to the silence

On Hyndford Street

Take me back, take me way, way, way back, on Hyndford
  Street
Where you could feel the silence at half past eleven on long
  summer nights
As the wireless played Radio Luxembourg and the voices
  whispered across Beechie River
In the quietness as we sank into restful slumber in the silence
  and carried on dreaming in God
And walks up Cherryvalley from North Road Bridge railway
  line on sunny summer afternoons
Picking apples from the side of the tracks that spilled over
  from the gardens of the houses on Cyprus Avenue
Watching the moth catcher work the floodlights in the
  evenings and meeting down by the pylons
Playing round Mrs Kelly's lamp, going out to Holywood on
  the bus
And walking from the end of the lines to the seaside,
  stopping at Fusco's for ice cream
In the days before rock 'n' roll
Hyndford Street, Abetta Parade, Orangefield, St Donard's
  Church
Sunday six bells and in between the silence there was
  conversation
And laughter and music and singing and shivers up the back
  of the neck
And tuning into Luxembourg late at night and jazz and blues
  records during the day
Also Debussy on the Third Programme, early mornings when
  contemplation was best
Going up the Castlereagh Hills and the Cregagh Glens in
  summer and coming back

To Hyndford Street, feeling wondrous and lit up inside, with
    a sense of everlasting life
And reading Mr Jelly Roll and Big Bill Broonzy and *Really
    the Blues* by Mezz Mezzrow
And *Dharma Bums* by Jack Kerouac, over and over again
And voices echoing late at night over Beechie River
And it's always being now, and it's always being now
It's always now. Can you feel the silence?
On Hyndford Street where you could feel the silence
At half past eleven on long summer nights
As the wireless played Radio Luxembourg and the voices
    whispered across Beechie River
And in the quietness we sank into restful slumber in silence
And carried on dreaming in God

Too Long in Exile

Too long in exile
Too long not singing my song
Too long in exile
Too long like a rolling stone
Too long in exile

Too long in exile
Baby, those people just ain't, just ain't your friends
Too long in exile, my friend
You can never go home again

Well, that isolated feeling
Drives you so close up against the wall
Till you feel like you can't go on
You've been in the same place for too long

Too long in exile
Baby, you can never go back home
Too long in exile
Any way you want

Oh that isolated feeling
Drives you up against, up against the wall
'Cause you've been on the mainland, baby
Been on the mainland, comin' on strong

Too long in exile
Too long people keep hanging on
Too long in exile
Too long like a rolling stone

And the wheeling and the dealing
All takes up too much time
Check your better self, baby
You'd better satisfy, satisfy your mind

Too long in exile
Too long you've been grinding at the mill
Too long in exile
Man, I've really just had my fill

Too long in exile
You can never go back home again
Too long in exile
Just about to drive me just insane

Too long in exile, been too long in exile
Just like James Joyce, baby
Too long in exile
Just like Samuel Beckett, baby
Too long in exile
Just like Oscar Wilde
Too long in exile
Just like George Best, baby
Too long in exile
Just like Alex Higgins, baby
Too long in exile

Wasted Years
(duet with John Lee Hooker)

Wasted years being brainwashed by lies
  Oh yes I have
Oh wasted years
  I'm talking about wasted years
Oh I'm not seeing eye to eye
  I just can't see the things I should see
Wasted years, baby
I was taking the wrong advice
  I know you was, I know you was
  And I was too

All alone I'm travelling
Travelling through these wasted years
  For so long, so long, so long I was
Oh I must have gained some wisdom
  Down through the years I did
Somewhere along the way
  Oh yes I did, oh yes I did
That's why there can't be no more
  No more
No more wasted years today
  I got wise, I got wise to myself

Well, baby, the great sadness
Oh you've got to let it all go
  Oh yeah, oh yeah, Van
Live in the present
Live in the future, Johnny, ain't that so?
  Oh it's a sad feeling, oh yeah
Oh you've gotta find something

To carry you through, carry you through
Carry you through

I've learned my lesson
I ain't gonna do it no more, yeah
Now, Van
Now, John
I've learned my lesson
I should have a long time ago
That's right
All these wasted years, wasted years
I finally woke up and got wise
I ain't gonna be, ain't gonna be no fool no more
Now, Van, now, Van
Ain't gonna be nobody's, 'body's fool no more
Sing the song, Van, sing it with me

Well, all alone, all alone I've been travelling
Travelling all alone through these wasted years
Dark, dark wasted years
So dark here
Dark, dark, dark, dark wasted years
I must have gained something
Oh travelling along the lonely way
Yeah, I've learned a lesson
I'm gonna make damn sure, baby, make damn sure
There's no more wasted years today

No Religion

We didn't know no better and they said it could be worse
Some people thought it was a blessing
Other people think that it's a curse
It's a choice between fact and fiction
And the whole world has gone astray
That's why there's no religion, no religion, no religion here
    today

And there's no straight answers
Of what this thing called love is all about
Some say it's unconditional
Other people just remain in doubt
When I cleaned up my diction, I had nothing left to say
Except there's no religion, no religion, no religion here today

And they ask what hate is, it's just the other side of love
Some people want to give their enemies
Everything they think that they deserve
Some say, 'Why don't you love your neighbour?
Go ahead and turn the other cheek'
But there's nobody on this planet that can ever be so meek
And I can't bleed for you, you have to do it your own way
And there's no religion, no religion, no religion here today

No religion, no religion, no religion here today

And they ask what hate is, it's the other side of love
Some people want to give their enemies
Everything they think that they deserve
Others say, 'Why don't you love your neighbour?
Go ahead and turn the other cheek'

Have you ever met anybody who'd ever been that meek?
And it's so cruel to expect the Saviour to save the day
And there's no religion, no religion, no religion here today

And there's no mystery and there's nothin' hidden
And there's no religion here today

And there's no mystery and there's nothin hidden
And there's no religion here today

And there's no religion, no religion, no religion here today

Songwriter

I'm a songwriter and I know just where I stand
I'm a songwriter, pen and paper in my hand
Get the words on the page
Please don't call me a sage
I'm a songwriter

I'm a songwriter and I do it for a living
I'm a songwriter and I write about men and women
I can write about love and the stars up above
I'm a songwriter

I'm a songwriter and I'm hot on your trail
I'm a songwriter and my cheque's in the mail
I can move with the scene, I can make up a dream
I'm a songwriter

I'm a songwriter, I can do it for certain
I'm a songwriter, even do it when I'm hurtin'
And if it comes to the bit, have to write another hit
I'm a songwriter

I'm a songwriter, I can put it in words
I'm a songwriter and it's not for the birds
I can spin you a yarn, it's as long as my arm
I'm a songwriter

I'm a songwriter
I'm a songwriter

Days Like This

When it's not always raining, there'll be days like this
When there's no one complaining, there'll be days like this
When everything falls into place like the flick of a switch
Well, my mama told me, there'll be days like this

When you don't need to worry, there'll be days like this
When no one's in a hurry, there'll be days like this
When you don't get betrayed by that old Judas kiss
Oh my mama told me, there'll be days like this

When you don't need an answer, there'll be days like this
When you don't meet a chancer, there'll be days like this
When all the parts of the puzzle start to look like they fit
Then I must remember, there'll be days like this

When everyone is upfront and they're not playing tricks
When you don't have no freeloaders out to get their kicks
When it's nobody's business the way that you wanna live
I just have to remember, there'll be days like this

When no one steps on my dreams, there'll be days like this
When people understand what I mean, there'll be days like
    this
When you ring out the changes of how everything is
Well, my mama told me, there'll be days like this

Oh my mama told me, there'll be days like this
Oh my mama told me, there'll be days like this
Oh my mama told me, there'll be days like this

Fire in the Belly

Call of the wildest, it's got the best of you
I got fire in my heart, fire in my belly too
Got a heart and a mind and a fire inside
And I'm crazy about you
You, you on your high-flying cloud
You, you when you're laughing out loud
You, you with your hidden surprise
You

Stoke up my engine, bring me my driving wheel
Once I get started, you'll know just how I feel
And I'm crazy about you
And I'm crazy about you
And I'm crazy about you
You, you on your high-flying cloud
You, you when you're laughing out loud
You, you with your hidden surprise
You

Gotta get through January
Gotta get through February
Gotta get through January
Gotta get through February
Gotta get through January
Gotta get through February
Gotta get through January

Spring in my heart, fire in my belly too
I come apart, I don't know just what to do
Got a heart and a mind and a fire inside
And I'm crazy about you

You, you on your high-flying cloud
You, you with the laugh in your eyes
You, you with your hidden surprise
You

Gotta get through January
Gotta get through February
Gotta get through January
Gotta get through February
Gotta get through January
Gotta get through February
Gotta get through January

Spring in my heart, fire in my belly too
I come apart, I don't know just what to do
I got a heart and a mind and a fire inside
And I'm crazy about you
You, you on your high-flying cloud
You, you with the laugh in your eyes
You, you with your hidden surprise
You

Talkin' 'bout you
Talkin' 'bout you
Talkin' 'bout you
Talkin' 'bout you
Talkin' 'bout you
Talkin' 'bout you, talkin' 'bout you
Talkin' 'bout you, fire in the belly too

Talkin' 'bout you, talkin' 'bout you
Talkin' 'bout you, talkin' 'bout you
Talkin' 'bout you, talkin' 'bout you
Talkin' 'bout you, talkin' 'bout you
Talkin' 'bout you, talkin' 'bout you
Talkin' 'bout you

Burning Ground

And I take you down to the burning ground
And you change me up and you turn it around
In the wind and rain I'm gonna see you again
In the morning sun and when the day is done
And you take my hand and you walk with me
And sometimes it feels like eternity
And I turn the tide, I get back my pride
And I make you proud when you say it out loud
When I you take you down to the burning ground
To the burning ground, to the burning ground
To the burning ground, to the burning ground

And I take you down by the factory
And I show you like it has to be
And you understand how the work is done
And I pick up the sack in the midday sun
And I pull you through by the skin of your teeth
And I lift the veil to see what's underneath
And you return to me and you sit on your throne
And you make me feel that I'm not alone
And I take you down to the burning ground
To the burning ground, to the burning ground
To the burning ground

Hey, man, who's that you're carrying?

Feels like lead

*It weighs a ton – let's see if we can dump it by the side of
the hill*

Hey, wait up, why don't you dump it on the burning ground?

Dump it down there

Yeah, man, dump the jute

Hey, man, dump the jute on the burning ground

Dump the jute?

Yeah, you know, dump the jute

Dump the jute!

On the burning ground
On the burning ground

And you make me think what it's all about
Sometimes I know, gonna work it out
And I watch you run in the crimson sun
Tear my shirt apart, open up my heart
And I watch you run down on your bended knees
By the burnt-out well, can you tell me please?
Between heaven and hell won't you take me down
To the burning ground, to the burning ground
To the burning ground, to the burning ground?

And you fall and pray, when you hear that sound
And we're walking back to the burial mound
And you shake your head and you turn it around
And you see the flames from the burning ground
And you get down on your knees and pray
And I catch my breath as we're running away
And I take the jute and I throw him down
On the burning ground, on the burning ground
On the burning ground, it's on the burning ground

Sometimes We Cry

Sometimes we know, sometimes we don't
Sometimes we give, sometimes we won't
Sometimes we're strong, sometimes we're wrong
Sometimes we cry

Sometimes it's bad when the going gets tough
Yet we look in the mirror and we want to give up
Sometimes we don't even think we'll try
Sometimes we cry

Well, we're gonna have to sit down and think it right through
If we're only human what more can we do?
The only thing to do is eat humble pie
Sometimes we cry

'Fore they put me in a jacket and they take me away
I'm not gonna fake it like Johnnie Ray
Sometimes we live, sometimes we die
Sometimes we cry

Sometimes we can't see anything straight
Sometimes everybody is on the make
Sometimes it's lonely on the lost highway
Sometimes we cry, sometimes we cry

Gonna put me in a jacket and take me away
I'm not gonna fake it like Johnnie Ray
Sometimes we live, sometimes we die
Sometimes we cry, sometimes we cry

Sometimes we live, sometimes we die
Sometimes we cry, sometimes we cry

[168]

Not Supposed to Break Down

You're not supposed to be human
You're not supposed to really feel
Not supposed to get involved with
Anything completely real
Fifteen families starving
All around the corner block
Here we're standing so alone
Just like Gibraltar Rock

Not supposed to break down
You're not supposed to break down
Swallow the dirt
Keep listening to the hurt
You'll be safe and sound

Supposed to be superhuman
Cover everything
Just like a bird
Cover an egg with its wing
And you know there's nothing sacred
But what is the use?
No point trying to find
What it's worth, what is true

Not supposed to break down
You're not supposed to break down
Swallow the hurt
Listen to the dirt
You'll be safe and sound

You're not supposed to break down

You're not supposed to break down
Swallow the hurt
Listen to the dirt
You'll be safe and sound

A fool and his mainline connection
Bypass going to the well
But that doesn't matter any more
I'm sure that we can tell
Who's a puppet on a string
And who really holds the glove
But it ain't up to you and me
It's up to the Lord above

You're not supposed to break down
You're not supposed to break down
Swallow the hurt
Keep on listening to the dirt
And I'll bet you'll be safe and sound

You're not supposed to break down
You're not supposed to break down
Swallow the hurt
Listen to the dirt
I'll bet you'll be safe and sound
And I'll bet you'll be safe and sound
And I'll bet you'll be safe and sound
I'll bet you'll be safe and sound

Madame Joy

All the men would turn their head
When she walked down the street
Clothes were fine and hair that shines
Smiling oh so sweet, smiling oh so sweet

Got a taste of old religion
Comes on with the new
In her hair a yellow ribbon
And she's decked out all in blue
Oh yes in, decked out all in blue

Steppin' lightly, steppin' brightly
With her books in hand
Going to the university to teach and
Help them understand
And help them understand

And all the kids would love to see her
Follow in her steps
And tell her stories and adore her
Climb in through the fence
Climb in through the fence

Here she comes walking
Here she comes talking
I do believe it's Madame Joy
Walking past that old street corner
And she's looking for her boy
Oh yes she is, looking for her boy

Steppin' lightly, steppin' brightly

With her books in hand
Going to the university to teach and
Help them understand
Help them understand

I was looking at the way she moved me
And I was seeing every sign
Tell me, can I learn the language?
Have you got the mind?
Have you got the mind?

Here she comes walking
Here she comes talking
I do believe it's Madame Joy
She's walking by that old street corner
And she's looking for her boy
Looking for her boy

And all the men would turn their head
When she walked down the street
Clothes refined and hair that shines
And smiling oh so sweet, oh yes, she's smiling oh so sweet
Smiling, smiling oh so sweet
Smiling, smiling oh so sweet

And all the men would
And all the men would turn their head around
When that woman walked down the street
When that woman walked down the street
When that, when that woman walked
When that woman walked, when that woman walked
When that woman walked, when that woman walked
When that woman walked, what she wore
When that woman, when that woman, when that woman
When that woman, when that woman, when that woman

When that woman, when that woman, when that woman
When that woman, when that woman walked
She just walked
Just kept on walking down the street
When she walked, when she walked down
When she walked on down

Naked in the Jungle

Naked in the jungle, naked to the world
Naked in the jungle, naked to the world
Well, you gotta keep it humble, else it'll come unfurled

Lions and the tigers, grazin' in the grass
Lions and the tigers, grazin' in the grass
There's a keeper watching over, make sure no one gets past

Speak out, speak out, speak out, speak out
Speak out, speak out, speak out, speak out
Speak out, speak out, speak out, speak out
Speak out, speak out, speak out, speak out

Big fish eat the little fish and the rabbit's on the run
Big fish eat the little fish and the rabbit's on the run
Some folks gettin' too much, others just ain't gettin' none

Naked in the jungle, naked to the world
Naked in the jungle, naked to the world
Well you gotta keep it humble, else it'll come unfurled

Let's go, boy
Speak out, speak out, speak out, speak out
Speak out, speak out, speak out, speak out
Speak out, speak out, speak out, speak out
Speak out, speak out, speak out, speak out

The Street Only Knew Your Name

Your street, rich street or poor
You should always be sure of your street
There's a place in your heart, when you know from the start
And you can't be complete without a street

Keep movin' on, just like a train
Sometimes you gotta look back to the street again
Would you prefer all those castles in Spain
Or a view of the street from your windowpane?

When you were young, so young
So very, very young
When you were young, so young
So very, very, very young
And the street only knew your name
And the street only knew your name
And the street only knew your name, oh your precious name,
    precious name

There was Walter and John, Katie and Ron
They all hung around the corner lamplight
Get together, sing some songs
Like 'Boppin' the Blues'
'You Make Me Feel Alright'

That was long before fortune and fame
No such thing as a star when you played that game
Everyone knew who everyone was
There was no pretence in the street, no, no

When you were young, so young

So very, very, very, very young
When you were young, so young
So very, very, very young
And the street only knew your name
And the street only knew your name
And the street only knew your name, oh your name, your
    precious name

And you walked around in the heart of town
Listening for that sound
And you walked around in the heart of town
Listening for that sound
'Blue Suede Shoes', it was the 'Blue Suede Shoes'

When you were young, so young
So very, very, very, very young
When you were young, so young
Very, very, very young
And the street only knew your name
And the street only knew your name
And the street only knew your name
Talking 'bout the street now, baby

We were singing 'Be-Bop-A-Lula'
We were singing 'Blue Suede Shoes'
We were singing 'Good Golly Miss Molly'
We were singing 'Tutti Frutti'
We were singing 'What'd I Say'
We were singing 'Boppin' the Blues' and 'Who Slapped
    John?'
When the street only knew your name
Talkin' about a funky street now, baby

And the street only knew your name

Show Business

Say you wanna be in show business
See the man on the TV with a phoney smile
Bring you up, bring you down
He can turn your head around
In show business, show business

See the man on a silver screen
With the phoney smile
Bring you up, bring you down
He can turn your head around
Show business, show business

Have a hit, maybe two
Make mincemeat out of you
Come back in two years' time
Lay your heart right on the line
In show business, show business
Show business, show business

Where's the next one, where's the next one?
Where's the next one?
Oh baby, just like the last one
Like the last one

Say you wanna be in show business
See the man in the suit
With the phoney smile
He can laugh, he can cry
He can make you reach the sky
He can say anything you wanna hear
Be anything you wanna be

He can say anything you want to hear
Be anything you want him to be
Make you leave your family
In show business, in show business

Take it to the bridge
And the next one and the next one
And the next one
Can you do it like the last one?
Now do it just like the last one, please
Like the last one, like the last one
Just like the last one

Say you wanna be in show business
Have a pretty face and a pretty smile
I'm thinking
Make you laugh and they can make you cry
But they can't wait, wipe the teardrops from your eye
In show business, show business

Say you wanna be in show business
See the rock star up on the stage
Right now
Behind them drugs, behind them booze
Behind them people he can use
Behind them people usin' them
Behind them people usin' us
And the next one and the next one
And the next one
Can you make it just like the last one?
Oh you make it just like the last one
Like the last one
Just like the last one

Say you wanna be in show business

All the world is a stage
Everybody must play their part
I've been so long in show business
I feel right now just like I got myself a start
Forget the junk, forget the jive
I just want to stay alive
In show business, in show business

Take it to the bridge
And the next one and the next one
And the next one
Oh just like the last one, just like the last one
Like the last one

Can I rob you with a fountain pen?
But you got to find some honest men
They can make you leave your home
Where you go to waste and roam
Control your fate, control your life
They can make you leave your wife
It's show business, it's show business

Take it to the bridge
And the next one and the next one
And the next one
Oh just like the last one
Can you make it
Like the last one?
Can you give it one more time
Like the last one?
Can you put it out like the last one?
Show business, it's show business
It's show business, show business
It's show business, show business
It's show business, show business

Philosopher's Stone

Out on the highways and the byways all alone
I'm still searching for, searching for my home
Up in the morning, up in the morning out on the road
And my head is aching and my hands are cold
And I'm looking for the silver lining, silver lining in the
    clouds
And I'm searching for
And I'm searching for the philosopher's stone

And it's a hard road, it's a hard road, daddy-o
When my job is turning lead into gold
He was born in the backstreet, born in the backstreet Jelly
    Roll
I'm on the road again and I'm searching for
The philosopher's stone
Can you hear that engine?
Oh can you hear that engine drone?
Well, I'm on the road again and I'm searching for
Searching for the philosopher's stone

Up in the morning, up in the morning
When the streets are white with snow
It's a hard road, it's a hard road, daddy-o
Up in the morning, up in the morning
Out on the job
Well, you've got me searching for
Searching for, the philosopher's stone
Even my best friends, even my best friends they don't know
That my job is turning lead into gold
When you hear that engine, when you hear that engine
    drone

I'm on the road again and I'm searching for the philosopher's
   stone

It's a hard road, even my best friends they don't know
And I'm searching for, searching for the philosopher's stone

High Summer

By the mansion on the hillside
A red sports car comes driving down the road
And pulls up into the driveway
And the story does unfold

She's standing by the rhododendrons
Where the roses are in bloom
Looking out at the Atlantic Ocean
And in her head she hums this tune

Thank God the dark nights are drawing in again
'Cause high summer has got me down
Have to wait till the end of August
And to get off this merry-go-round

And they shut him out of paradise
Called him Lucifer and frowned
'Cause he took pride in what God made him
Even before the angels shot him down to the ground

He's a light out of the darkness
And he wears a starry crown
If you see him, nothin's shakin'
'Cause high summer has got him low down

High summer's got him lonesome
Even when he makes the rounds
There's been no two ways about it
High summer's got him low down

Checked into the tiny village by the lakeside

Settled down to start anew
Far away from the politicians
And the many chosen few

Far away from the jealousy factor
And everything that was tearing him apart
Far away from the organ grinder
And everyone that played their part

And they shut him out of paradise
Called him Lucifer and frowned
'Cause he took pride in what God made him
Even before the angels shot him to the ground

He's a light out of the darkness
And he wears a starry crown
If you see him nothin's shakin'
High summer's got him low down

High summer's on the rebound
High summer's got him low down
High summer's on the rebound
High summer's got him low down
High summer's on the rebound
High summer's got him low down
Low down

Choppin' Wood

You wired the trains and went back home to St Clair Shores
Before you became a spark down at the yard
You were passing through those hungry years alone
You were just trying to make a living out in Detroit

When you came back off the boats you didn't want to go
    anywhere
You sit down to TV in your favourite chair
You watched the big picture fade away down at Harland and
    Wolff
But you still kept on choppin' wood

And you came back home to Belfast
So you could be with us *like*
You lived a life of quiet desperation on the side
Going to the shipyard in the morning on your bike

Well, the spark was gone but you carried on
You always did the best you could
You sent for us once but everything fell through
But you still kept on choppin' wood, choppin' wood

Well, you came back home to Belfast
So you could be with us *like*
And you lived a life of quiet desperation on the side
Going to the shipyard in the morning on your bike

Well, the spark was gone but you carried on
Well, you did just the best that you could
You sent for us one time but everything fell through
But you still kept on choppin' wood

Kept on choppin' wood
Kept on choppin' wood
Local man chops wood
You know you did the best you could

Well, everything just fell through
Kept on choppin' wood
Chop, chop, chop, chop, chop
Chop, chop, chop, chop, chop
Chop, chop, chop, keep on choppin'
Chop, chop, chop, choppin' wood

What Makes the Irish Heart Beat

All that trouble, all that grief
That's why I had to leave
Staying away too long is in defeat
Why I'm singing this song
When I'm heading back home
That's what makes the Irish heart beat

I'm just like a hobo riding a train
I'm like a gangster living in Spain
Have to watch my back and I'm running out of time
Well, I'll roll the dice again
If Lady Luck will call my name
That's what makes the Irish heart beat

Well, that's what makes it beat
When I'm standing on the street
And I'm standing underneath this Wrigley's sign
Oh so far away from home
But I know I've got to roam
That's what makes the Irish heart beat

And it was off to foreign climes
On the Piccadilly line
We were standing underneath the Wrigley's sign
So far away from home
Well, I know I've got to roam
That's what makes the Irish heart beat

Just like a sailor out on the foam
Any port in a storm
When we tend to burn the candle at both ends

Down the corridors of fame
Like the spark ignites the flame
That's what makes the Irish heart beat

But I'll roll the dice again
If Lady Luck will call my name
That's what makes the Irish heart beat
Oh that's what makes the Irish heart beat
That's what makes the Irish heart beat

What's Wrong with This Picture?

What's wrong with this picture?
There's something I'm not seeing here
What's wrong with this picture?
Something's not exactly clear

What's wrong with this picture?
Does it look like it's just another sting, sting?
'Cause it don't mean a thing
If it ain't got that swing and ring a ding ding

What's wrong with this picture?
Doesn't anybody see
That's who everyone thought
That I used to be?

What's wrong with this picture?
It's only just hanging on a wall
So you can go right back to sleep
And just forget about it all, because

I'm not that person any more
I'm living in the present time
Baby, don't you understand
I've left all that jive behind

You can't believe what you read in the papers
Or half the news that's on TV
Or the gossip of the neighbours
Or anyone who doesn't want you to be free

I'm not that person any more

I'm always living in the present time
Don't you understand?
I left all that jive behind

What's wrong with this picture?
It's only hanging on the wall
Why don't we take it down and
Just forget about it 'cause that ain't me at all?

Somerset

We met deep down in Somerset
A time I can't forget
When we were sippin' cider in the shade

Oh the sun was setting in the west
You looked your very best that night
Stars were shining in your eyes

And we walked, walked all along the sand
And it felt, felt like a wonderland

And when the summer breeze was gone
The memory lingered on
You and me down in Somerset

Oh we walked, walked and walked and walked all along the
    sand
And it felt just like our love just began

And when the summer breeze was gone
The memory lingered on, me and you
When the summer set

We met, we met, we met deep down in Somerset
A time I can't forget
You were sippin' cider in the shade

Meaning of Loneliness

Lost in a strange city, nowhere to turn
Far cry from the streets that I came from
It can get lonely when you're travelling hard
But you can even be lonely standing in your own backyard

Nobody knows the existential dread
Of the things that go on inside someone else's head
Whether it be trivial or something that Dante said
But, baby, nobody knows the meaning of loneliness

No matter how well you know someone you can only ever
    guess
How can you ever really know somebody else?
It takes more than a lifetime just to get to know yourself
Nobody knows the meaning of loneliness

I have to say a word about solitude
For the soul it, sometimes they say, can be good
And I'm partial to it myself, well, I must confess
Nobody knows the meaning of loneliness

Well, there's Sartre and Camus, Nietzsche and Hesse
If you dig deep enough you gonna end up in distress
And no one escapes having to live life under duress
And no one escapes the meaning of loneliness

Well, they say keep it simple when it gets to be a mess
And fame and fortune never brought anyone happiness
I must be lucky, some of my friends think that I'm really
    blessed
Nobody knows the meaning of loneliness

No, no, no, no, no, no, nobody knows the meaning of
   loneliness
No, no, no, no, nobody knows the meaning of loneliness
Nobody knows the meaning of loneliness

Stranded

I'm stranded at the edge of the world
It's a world I don't know
Got nowhere to go
Feels like I'm stranded

And I'm stranded between that ol' devil and the deep blue sea
Ain't nobody's gonna tell me
Tell me what, what time it is

Every day, every day, it's hustle, hustle time, hustle time
Every day and every way, one more, one more mountain to
    climb

It's leaving me stranded in my own little island
With my eyes open wide
But I'm feeling stranded

Every, every, every day, it's hustle time
Every way, one more mountain to climb

I'm stranded between the devil and the deep blue sea
There ain't nowhere else to be
'Cept right here and I'm stranded

Pay the Devil

One man's meat is another man's poison
One man's gain can be another man's loss
I'm travelling down the lonely highway
'Cause a rolling stone don't gather no moss

Once I thought I could live the kind of life I wanted
But the wayward wind made me restless and a fool of me
'Cause I thought I could settle for the nine-to-five life
Well, I guess it just was never meant to be

Now people talk and they speculate about what other people
   would do
But they can't put themselves within my shoes
It used to be my life, now it's become my story
I'm heading down this highway with those blues

Well, I'd love to see the sun setting on the riverside
Just to go back home and I want to settle down
Well, I have to pay the devil for my music
Why I have to keep on with this roaming around?

Have to pay the devil for my music
Keep on rolling from town to town
Have to pay the devil for to play my music
Keep on rolling from town to town

This Has Got to Stop

I've given you my heart and my soul
I've given you more than you'll ever know
I've given you just about everything I can
Can't you see that I'm just only one man?

I took you out to the picture show
Then I took you walkin' outdoors
I walked you up and down the block
Then I warned you, 'Baby, this has got to stop'

This has got to stop, you're way over the top
Pack my things and walk, we can't even talk
This has got to stop, I just had enough
I'm gonna call your bluff, walk you one more lap

And I watched you watching me as I watched you walk away
    from me
And I went off to that far country
I took a plane out to that Newfoundland
When you said to me that you didn't understand

This has got to stop, you're way over the top
I'm gonna pack my things and walk, we don't even talk
This has got to stop, baby, I just had enough
I'm gonna call your bluff, walk me one more lap

Well, I came back home and I burnt our house down
I watched it crumble to the ground
Oh it caved in like a piece of balsa wood
I turned to you and said, 'Baby, this is just no good'

And I worked and I tried to build it all back up again
The day you told me that you had really changed
Then you knocked down all my castles in the sand
Then I said, 'Baby, I know now just where we stand'

This has got to stop, you're way over the top
Pack my bags and walk, we don't even talk
This has got to stop, I've just had enough
I'm gonna call your bluff, this has got to stop

This has got to stop
Stop, stop, I've had enough
I'm gonna call your bluff
Stop, stop, stop
This has got to stop

End of the Land

When too many demands have destroyed all my plans
Going down to the end of the land
If I have to drive all night just to feel alright
Going down to the end of the land

When it gets out of hand and I fail to agree
Just what's in it for me?
Going down to the sea

Then I've got to run towards the setting sun
Going down to the end of the land

When it gets out of hand and I beg to disagree
Just what's in it for me?
Get back down to the sea

And then I've got to run to the setting sun
Going down to the end of the land
If I've got to drive all night till the morning light
I'm going down to the end of the land

Going down, going down, going down to the end of the land
Going down to the end of the land

Song of Home

Well, it's written in the wind
For the story does begin
I will go back to my kin across the sea
There's a bird that's on the wing and it's flying free
He can hear the song of home endlessly

Well, the further I must go
Then the nearer I must stay
Men have sailed the seven seas to be free
And like that bird that's on the wing and is flying free
He can hear the song of home endlessly

I can see the harbour lights
Hear the foghorns in the night
All up and down the lough, calling

From the rocky shores of Maine
I will sail back home again
Back to where my heart longs to be
And the bird that's on the wing and is flying free
He can hear the song of home endlessly

I can see the harbour lights
Hear the foghorns in the night
Boats up and down the lough, calling, calling

From the rocky shores of Spain
I will sail back home again
Back to where my heart will always be
Just like a bird that's on the wing and is flying free
He can hear the song of home endlessly

He can hear the song of home endlessly
He can hear the song of home endlessly

Soul

Soul is a feeling, feeling deep within
Soul is not the colour of your skin
Soul is the essence, essence from within
It is where everything begins

Soul is what you've been through
What's true for you
Where you going to
What you're gonna do

Soul is your station or the folk of your nation
Something that you wear with pride
Soul can be your vision or something that is hidden
It's not something that you gotta hide

Soul is what you've been through
And what's true for you
Where you going to
What you're gonna do

Soul can be your station or the folk of your nation
Something that you wear with pride
Soul can be your vision, it can be your religion
Something that you just can't hide

Soul is a feeling, feeling deep within
Soul is not the colour of your skin
Soul is the essence, essence from within
Soul is where everything begins

Mystic of the East

Mystic of the East, mystic from the streets
Mystic with no brief, back here on the street
Mystic out of reach, can't find no reason to speak
I just got in too deep for the mystic of the East

I was deep in the heart of Down
Deep in the heart of Down
Deep in the heart of Down
Deep in the heart

Mystic with no peace, back here in the East
Fed up to the teeth, mystic of the East

I was deep in the heart of Down
Deep in the heart of Down
Deep in the heart of Down
Deep in the heart

Mystic out of reach, can't seem to find my brief
Gone with the wild geese and I've had it up to the teeth
Mystic of the East, back here on the streets
Mystic with no brief, I can't find any reason to speak

Mystic of the East, East, East, East
Back here on the street, back on the street
Back on the street, mystic of the East
Back here on the street, mystic of the East

Acknowledgements

Many thanks to Lee and all those at Faber for their belief in this book. Thanks also to Eamonn and Ian.

I would like to acknowledge my assistant Kerry Adamson for making sure all the loose ends got tied up, the corrections got done and for the project finally coming to fruition.

Index of Titles and First Lines

Song titles are in italic; first lines are in roman